PRAISE FOR *MARIA ANTONIA Y SUS RETOÑOS:*
LEGACIES OF MOTHERHOOD

"Maria Antonia's life is anything but ordinary.
In her quest to live reasonably, her unrelinquished
dignity and compassion reminds us that in the
creases of abuela's wrinkles are mapped the stories
of hard-won victories and mistakes, cares remembered
and forgotten, and, most importantly, the spirit
of tenacity that crafts a lifetime."

—ROBERTA HURTADO, PH.D.
Director, Latino and Latin American Studies,
State University of New York at Oswego

CONOCIMIENTOS
PRESS

Maria Antonia y sus retoños

Legacies of Motherhood

ROSIE CARBÓ

CONOCIMIENTOS

PRESS

Book design by ash good.

Published by Conocimientos Press, LLC
San Antonio, Texas

ISBN: 978-1-961-794-05-4

CONOCIMIENTOSPRESSLLC.COM

In loving memory of my grandmother

Maria Antonia Menchaca

1901–2007

PRELUDE

WITH *Maria Antonia y sus retoños: Legacies of Motherhood,* we are transported in and out of an extraordinary life. As parallel travelers, Rosie Carbó unfolds her abuela's life. Like a rose with many off-shoots, Maria Antonia connects her beloved grandchildren's lives to the daily experiences of survival. As one of those sprouts, the author narrates their shared experiences through memories, journal entries, and oral histories captured from abuela, to bring forth well-lived lives, despite the hardships her family confronted to survive. In some cases, to give her family privacy, Carbó relays these stories using psuedonyms for living family members.

—JOSIE MÉNDEZ-NEGRETE, *EDITOR*

PREFACE

PRESIDENT GEORGE W. BUSH never met Maria Antonia Menchaca. Perhaps, if he had he would have bestowed her the Presidential Medal of Freedom for love of country and family. Being one-hundred-and-six and remaining free of life-altering diseases, shaped her as an extraordinary woman, especially because of her mental capabilities. This aptitude surprised everyone who knew her. From her, I would learn the ways of family and patriotism.

Her spirit was that of an old soul. However, this was not a persona she embodied until much later.

After celebrating her fifty-fifth birthday, Maria Antonia began to embrace her senior citizen status. This was when the auburn hair color shifted into a thick, fluffy mass, resembling those white cotton blobs that are unceremoniously shoved into bottles of aspirins, which she was known to rely on for her pains.

I still remember the ruby red grapefruit color of her scalp framing her face because of those dyeing days. Interestingly, her white hair bordered a wrinkled face that made her appearance striking. Thinking back, I have come to realize that it was my intervention that made her stop coloring her hair. It was that time she asked whether she should color it.

No abuelita. Me gusta mucho su color plata.

I loved her silver hair and said so. Those words were enough for abuela to not dye her hair ever again. Even if she went against the objection of her only daughter—my mother, Minerva Menchaca Castañeda.

Abuelita was a great influence on me, representing all that my own mother was not. Unlike my own mother, Maria Antonia was loving and demonstrative. She would even share her own wardrobe with us. Often, she wore a blue cotton dress with buttons down the middle—her beloved batas—that freed her from bodily constraints. They allowed her to cope with the heat. In those airy tent dresses, we could be comfortable.

A smile comes to my face, when I recall the meaning of those garments. When we visited, every one of her granddaughters were instructed to "vete al ropero y coje una de tantas batas." We did as she told us. With a "sí abuelita," we affirmed the mandate and put on the housecoats for the duration of our visit. This was not something my mother would have ever done. Abuelita's warm brown eyes and her loving voice were most memorable for us grandchildren.

—ROSIE CARBÓ, 2025

In Michigan, the family arrived each in their own time, to celebrate abuela's birthday. Minerva, came to the nursing home, hoping to hear about friendly staff and new friends, but abuela only said *sácame de aquí*—ever determined to be discharged from the nursing home so she could go back to her precious San Antonio house, where she had planned to spend the rest of her life. Maria Antonia repeated, "Minerva, sácame de aquí."

She had been in the Michigan nursing home for several months and never stopped asking her daughter to take her out of there. Since Maria Antonia never learned to speak English, the mother and daughter spoke Spanish. Whatever language it was didn't matter; they never listened to each other anyway. And so, words would fly in either direction without engaging the meanings that were expressed.

Soon, Maria Antonia stopped listening to her daughter.

Despite excitement expressed by the family over the upcoming birthday party and a new haircut, Maria Antonia only wanted answers as to why she couldn't live in her own home rather than at a Texas mandated facility.

"¡Sácame de aquí, Minerva!"

There it was again the dog was pulling that bone. Maria Antonia demanded to go home. Minerva tried to change the direction of her words. All she could say was, "Toña, your haircut looks like short-grained rice."

No one listened. No one heard Maria Antonia's wish to go home.

Since the nursing home staff knew very little about the newly arrived resident, they heaped on compliments over the new eye-catching do. Yet those who knew the feisty, independent centenarian realized that the haircut was another indignity on a long list of many insults. All these were mortifications that could have explained why Maria Antonia was sullen and to herself—after all birthdays were to survive, not to celebrate. Still, seated in the wheelchair, Maria Antonia was the picture of vitality. Her health and her age were unique. However, her lucidity was the real mystery to everyone around her.

At the nursing home, they woke her up at seven in the morning to report to breakfast. Never an early riser, and not one to socialize with strangers, if she wanted to eat breakfast she had to comply. Why should she get up? No one spoke Spanish or tried to reach out to her. She was also required to do daily physical exercises, which called for alternating leg lifts—something she had never done in her life. All the exercise she did was fieldwork when she guided her family in their migratory work or when she tended to the garden. Of course, she strongly objected, and found it extremely a waste of time and unnecessary. In her San Antonio home, she relied on chairs as modes of transportation, as these gave her the support she needed, thus turning them into walkers when she needed to get from point one to point two. She never fell and was always confident of the space in which she walked.

Maria Antonia experienced profound indignation about losing her independence. She had always been in total control of her life as well as the lives of her family. She stood by them regardless of the consequences. Whenever the staff at the facility groomed her, she strongly objected to manicures or pedicures. With an uproarious laugh, Maria Antonia explained her non-cooperation.

> The trouble with getting old is that people think all your wrinkles, your veins, and your worn-out joints mirror your mind. But when I lived in my home, I used to talk to younger people all the time. I'd asked them questions they couldn't answer. And, many-a-time, I already knew the answer. So, I think I outwitted them.

Maria Antonia was keenly aware that months had passed since she was forced out of her home in Texas and pushed into a squalid nursing home. Some months later, a Texas court order granted her a transfer to Michigan. In that coordinated plot to move Maria Antonia, her life had been turned upside down. It happened so fast, that for Maria Antonia, it was a bad dream. The more days passed, the more she came to terms that this was her new reality.

MARIA ANTONIA awoke in a strange bed. The first thing she saw was another woman in a twin-sized bed across from her. This was an unusual situation, she had always been fearless, unafraid to try her hand at anything, including laying a cement floor in her basement. But falling down a flight of stairs and hurting her thigh resulted in years of pain and trouble walking—when her only relief were countless bottles of aspirins. She feared ending up in a nursing home. This was especially the case when the ambulance was called to her old, dilapidated home without air conditioning. Still, in fear of being institutionalized, Maria Antonia refused treatment. She would shout out.

"Esta es mi casa. ¡Quiero quedarme aquí hasta que Dios me recoja!"

The day she dreaded for years, happened. Strangers would take control of her life. Even the granddaughter she had not seen in thirty years was a stranger to her. And she would become her legal guardian. The person in charge of making decisions for abuela was Hilda Zonlak, a sweet granddaughter she had once cradled in her arms.

With the stroke of a pen, a family court judge in Texas appointed Hilda Zonlak as Maria Antonia's guardian. She willingly and graciously assumed the responsibility and often said,

> There was no one in the family who could take on this responsibility. As his child, I had to step up to the plate. My dad, Jeorge Castañeda was in a wheelchair. I had to do this for him, so I did it for abuelita so she could be close to family.

When she and her brother George Castañeda Jr. and their cousin Ana López saw the decrepit nursing home in San Antonio which their grandmother was forced into, they decided to hire a lawyer to get her out and transfer her to Michigan. Had they not prevailed, she would've died from neglect.

Through the work of an attorney, the judge remanded Maria Antonia to a nursing home in Frankenmuth. Maria Antonia was advised about the move and was happy to hear she would be near her family. However, she didn't understand the ramifications of that decision, unaware of the impending loss of her Texas home.

Throughout her life, Maria Antonia led by example. She showed her children that she could fend for herself. Did not leave anything to chance. Like clockwork, she paid her property taxes and utilities. Did everything she could to ensure she'd spend her final days in her own home. Now, everything from looming end-of-life decisions to personal hygiene were decided by her granddaughter.

Hilda, who was married and the mother of three, with a daughter who was hairdresser, decided Maria Antonia needed a haircut. However, when one of her granddaughters saw it, she said, "But, why so short?"

Hilda, who called her abuelita like all the grandchildren, defended her decision: "I didn't tell them to chop it off! I just thought it was time abuelita got a new hairstyle. I wanted her to have a new look for her upcoming birthday party." Someone in the visiting area called out.

"By the way, have you seen her toenails? They're so thick it'll take a veterinarian instrument to cut them." Somewhat defensively, Hilda offered.

"I asked the staff about bringing in someone to give abuelita her first-ever manicure and pedicure. But when I touched her fingernails and pointed to her toes, she said."

"No, No, No. ¿Para qué?"

Maria Antonia had never been catered to this way. Anyone who knew her or had given her a haircut knew the task was a major accomplishment. As one who long struggled to survive hardships, Maria Antonia had no need for such luxuries.

Maria Antonia's appearance was connected to the birthday party being planned with help of nursing home staff. Minerva, and some of her adult children who lived in Michigan, would arrive early to decorate the ballroom. Also, Maria Antonia's two aging sons, their spouses, children and grandchildren would join a host of friends. Maria Antonia's cousin, who migrated to the United States during Mexico's revolution, was also expected.

Minerva informed her mother that a family friend had reached out to the White House, to ask for a letter in recognition of her birthday, pointing to the envelope. "Toña, mira, this letter was sent to you from the White House. Es del Presidente Bush y su esposa Laura." Minerva who called her mother Toña, instead of mamá or mother, told her.

Unimpressed, Maria Antonia looked down at the letter, while examining it in silence. In her desire to point out the importance of her day, Minerva insisted, "The President of the United States and his wife want to wish you a happy birthday. It is not every day a person reaches your age. You are unique, Toña, because you're one hundred-and-four!" With that, Minerva opened the envelope and showed Maria Antonia the accompanying photo of the presidential couple.

Impressed by the letter, Minerva emphasized, "Que suerte tienes que se acuerden de ti. How lucky you are that they remembered you."

Minerva's words triggered an immediate and unexpected response from Maria Antonia.

"I can't believe the president sent me this letter and that picture. You're always trying to trick me, Minerva."

As she examined the photo of President and Mrs. Bush, while shaking her head slowly in disbelief, Maria Antonia showed her skepticism and mistrust of her daughter's words.

> Why would the president remember me? He does not even know me. If it's true, and you're not trying to make a fool out of me, show me the envelope addressed to me. If it really came de la Casa Blanca—the White House—the envelope will have the president's seal and return address. Show it to me!

Maria Antonia Menchaca had never been gullible. She had always been suspicious of strangers and even some relatives, and her daughter was no exception. Over the years, the mother and daughter had often argued about one thing or another.

Maria Antonia had a rock-solid determination. As Minerva had often been told, this character trait surfaced when her mother was an eight-year-old girl hellbent on riding the wild horse her father had given her. To make her point, Minerva pestered Maria Antonia by bringing out that story about the time she tamed that wild horse.

> My father didn't know the horse he gave me was so wild.
> When he saw the horse had a mind of its own, he wanted
> to sell it. He thought the rebel horse would hurt me, but
> I was determined to keep it. It took time and patience to
> tame him. I used a whip at first, but when he saw I meant
> business, I finally won the horse over.

Abuela proudly shared this childhood memory with all her children. Horseback riding was her passion at a time in which few if any automobiles were available or affordable in a Mexico that was dominated by a dictator and foreign investors. This was also a time in which most of Mexico's largest businesses were owned by the United States, Germans, and other foreigners. If those elite people couldn't fool abuela, how could Minerva hoodwink her? Maria Antonia wanted everyone to know her as a strong woman, often bringing up things that most mattered to her.

Horseback riding fed Maria Antonia's rebellious spirit and made her feel free. Horseback riding made her feel as free as the birds she fed at a pond on her father's ten-acre ranch. Her early years on the expansive homestead instilled in her the belief that animals were not meant to be caught and caged. She had decided long ago that the goats, cows, sheep, and horses she helped care for would roam freely on semi-green pastures. Horseback riding-bareback style was her favorite pastime. It was a privilege she earned through daily chores, which kept her too busy as a child.

Maria Antonia was as gentle and interested in flowers and trees as she was in her love of animals. And, while she loved horses more than any animal, she would never have a horse again in her future or adult life in the United States. She could not have envisioned the trappings of marriage. While a local boy caught her attention, for her marriage would have felt like she had been caught and caged. However, marriage and destiny took her far from her roots. Hard times made her long for her carefree upbringing before Mexico's Revolution. For Maria Antonia, there would be more disillusionments and much pain.

For instance, days before her secret teenage love finally gathered the courage to ask permission from her aunts to court her—Esteban Ruiz was killed in a farming accident. They met at her fifteenth quinceañera party with strict supervision of the aunts at their home. After a year of exchanging love notes, Maria Antonia was certain she had found the love of her life. Sadly, his untimely death sent her into a deep depression, and at the age of sixteen, she simulated the image of a grieving widow to the extreme of doing a novena and wearing black for an entire year.

After a year of mourning, Manuel Castañeda knocked at the door one summer morning. A tall, dark, forty-year-old widower, with a seven-year-old boy and five-year-old girl to raise, showed up at their doorstep. His position as the main bookkeeper of the local American-owned mining company held the promise of security and a bright future for abuela.

In Mexico it was not unusual for a seventeen-year-old teenager to marry a much older man. The older a bridegroom, the more likely family and friends saw the marriage as safe. Thus, love took a backseat to safety, poverty, and starvation.

Inside the culture, virginity was treasured and at a premium—Maria Antonia's chastity was coveted for this respectable fact. Still, she had a choice. She could have refused to marry Manuel Castañeda. Her father, Roque Menchaca, would have never insisted. And, if he had, she would've objected. The loss of her true love compelled Maria Antonia to accept the proposal. Despite her decision to marry, Maria Antonia never told anyone that she loved her husband. She simply offered that they got along fine regardless of personality and generational differences.

To the best of the family's recollection, Maria Antonia rarely mentioned the death of Esteban Ruiz, instead she beguiled her grandchildren with stories of a hypnotic waterfall that flowed from a mountain near Muzquiz, Coahuila. She painted the vast Mexican state as one that endured harsh winters and sizzling summers— paletas y caldos. That was the place where Maria Antonia spent her happiest years as a youngster, playing with her cousins near the beautiful and alluring waterfall, as she navigated the desert's heat. It was in her beloved Muzquiz that the spirited Maria Antonia roamed freely, unaware that Mexico's Revolution was simmering like a pot boiling over a stove.

Mounted atop Pedro, her horse, Maria Antonia tossed her head back in unbridled laughter. That horse filled her with joy and her father showered her with love. During those times, peasants who worked for hacendados began to challenge a system that consigned them to low peonage wages and poverty. Maria Antonia and her father had been right in the path of its genesis, when the country exploded as the landless masses joined to displace the landed gentry and the wealthy of the nation. The time came when deep-seated anger exploded into a bloody revolution.

She was only nine when it began. Maria Antonia's carefree world dramatically changed. The Mexican Revolution spread like wildfire throughout the country. La Revolución laid out a desperate fate for millions of Mexicans, ushering years of fear and upheaval. To anyone who listened, Maria Antonia would compare her perspective to those who wanted to return.

Many Mexicans who live here—in the United States— now say they want to return. But when I left with my husband, his children, and our two, I never wanted to return to Mexico. I remember so many people living in fear of being killed or dying of starvation. I'll never forget how helpless we felt then.

At the Texas border, with her husband Manual Castañeda and all their children, Maria Antonia started her own cafe in Nuevo Laredo, before entering the United States.

When they had saved enough money to survive, they crossed the border, dreaming about San Antonio, where they would later settle. The family began their new life free of disruptions from the revolution.

As creative and imaginative as she was, Maria Antonia would not ever have imagined her migration story. In a conversation with her granddaughter Anita, abuela recalled,

> We thought San Antonio would be the perfect place for us to start a new life. This was a town with a large Spanish-speaking population. What we found instead was widespread discrimination. Manuel had no choice but to take menial jobs—there was nothing else for him. We lived in San Antonio only two years until we moved to Dallas which we thought might be better.

In Dallas, Maria Antonia found work as a seamstress and milliner. Those skills got her hired making hats for the fashion-conscious high society of Dallas—she blessed the day her aunts taught her to sew.

She and her family would soon confront greater obstacles. Yet, the Great Depression took them by surprise. Along with many others, they lost their jobs. Not one to be readily defeated, Maria Antonia quickly found temporary work in a dress factory. Her husband, on the other hand, didn't try hard enough to find work. Similarly to the good worker who's looking for work and hoping not to find it, Manuel remained complacent. He spent hours reading and was satisfied with that, refusing to accept jobs other than that of a bookkeeper. His laziness and arrogance, fueled by lack of ambition produced many arguments between them. Sometime soon,

Manuel and his two grown children vanished. The marriage lasted twelve years and produced four children.

Left with no other option, Maria Antonia worked as never before, joining the migratory work force, and she and her children became laborers. These experiences were problematic for all. Still, abuela would often speak about the work ethic her sons developed because of their migrations.

> My sons grew up to be hard workers. Unlike other mothers whose children brought them problems, my sons had a strong work ethic and stayed out of trouble. Although my daughter hated and derided that backbreaking labor, my sons never complained about migratory work.

Among Maria Antonia's children, her three sons respected her—right or wrong. They listened and through their teenage years took her advice as they became responsible adult men. Her sole regret and something she never imagined was that her oldest son would denounce her later in life.

> When they did backbreaking work by my side, I never failed to give them the money they earned. I wanted to be fair. At a young age that money taught them that hard work paid off. All my children learned that trabajo y sudor—work and sweat—brought them great rewards.

Now, residing in a nursing home because of her legal guardianship, Maria Antonia showed to be more introspective and often reflected on her formative years in Mexico. She blamed a corrupt government for her situation and often talked about despising Mexico's politicians and its middle-class snobs. She blamed all of them for the upheaval and dislocation of millions of Mexicans during and after the revolution.

Even though, she arrived on the shores of the Rio Bravo after the revolutionary war ended, ghostly images of bloodied campesinos remained lodged in her mind. She often pictured a wave of humanity fleeing Mexico on horseback, a few in their Model T cars, but mostly on foot, like she and her family.

Her life experiences allowed Maria Antonia to embrace a philosophy of survival; that was all that mattered. Her lifelong preoccupation with food and shelter guided her every decision. To her, buying land and a house was the most important expenditure—owning real estate was as crucial as air and water.

The way she saw it, female desires, such as the latest fashion, manicures, pedicures, makeup and hairstyles, were for the upper class. Her mission was to live reasonably. Inside these beliefs, Maria Antonia confused feminine desire for improvement, seeing them as egotism, hedonism, and narcissism. She often told her teenaged granddaughters,

> Young, pretty girls hold their mirrors as a prized possession. Makeup, lipstick, and hair are important to girls your age. These things are unimportant. Beware of being self-engaged, because the need to work to survive melts away our vanity and drains our egos.

Based on the traditional beliefs found in Mexican culture, it was not at all unusual for a grandmother to look after her grandchildren. As such, Maria Antonia happily slid into the caretaker role. For nearly twenty years she tended to her son Jeorge's seven children. Abuela also became involved in the rearing of additional grandchildren, particularly her daughter's three oldest girls, Mercedes, Martha, and Anita.

In the late 1940s, all but her oldest son Francisco "Paco" Castañeda settled in Saginaw, a small Michigan town. Circumstances and fate sealed the family's destiny, even before her son Jeorge met and married Gregoria "Gloria" Zapata, who would be called Gloria. That was the time Maria Antonia purchased a one-story rural home, while Jeorge was a soldier in World War II and Korea. He was born in Texas and was extremely patriotic.

By the time her son returned, Maria Antonia had bought a larger, two-story home. The home was in the heart of burgeoning Saginaw, Michigan, near downtown, where she found a job as a dishwasher in a German bakery. For two decades, the white wood-clasped home was an anchor for Maria Antonia and her extended family. She told everyone near or far, "La casa chiquita fue una bendición!"

That small house was a blessing. It gave her teenage son, Beto, a chance to stay in school where he met his future wife. Too young to be drafted into the military, he helped his mother. The second home abuela bought was when Jeorge returned from the war, where he married and brought his young bride, and where all his children were conceived. The huge white house, with a half-acre backyard, was where Maria Antonia told stories about growing up in Mexico.

Her memories of the revolution were vivid and intact, and her storytelling was colorful and intriguing, often inspiring some family members. The one most motivated by her stories was Anita, her third oldest granddaughter, who would never forget abuela telling her:

> When my father took me to live with his two sisters, they insisted I help with chores. During our rare free time, they taught me to sew, embroider, crochet, cook, bake, and tend to the vegetable garden. They believed these skills would help me in the future.

Moralejas, or inherent values, embedded in the stories Maria Antonia told served her grandchildren well, and they listened attentively. Abuela often said,

> Life in a small town in Mexico was not easy. My aunts taught me to retain my pride and dignity in the face of hard times. They showed me not be ashamed of our lives. After all, it was our hard work that enabled us to sacar la familia adelante … get the family ahead, to buy land, a home, or whatever material possessions were necessary.

At the drop of a hat, and somewhat shifting the conversation, abuela continued explaining the ways of life in Muzquiz, recalling work inside and outside the house.

> In the chores our tías carried out and through their example, they taught me much early on. Even while dressed in voluminous enaguas petticoats and long, floor-length

skirts, they were not ashamed to pick up whatever implement was necessary to work in their vegetable garden or mount a horse when they had to. Despite hard times and hard work, my aunts retained their dignity and femininity.

Under their tutelage and supportive of her philosophy that hard work is honorable and good, Maria Antonia learned to embrace hard work. For her, work was the compass that guided her life. Her ravaged hands and prematurely aged face remained evidence of hard work. She took in Anita's quizzical look, and Abuela continued, "I wasn't always an old lady. There was a time I also was young."

Anita, who had learned to speak Spanish as a child, was able to understand her every word. Still, to ensure she did not lose a thing about what abuelita was talking, Anita translated the narrative she carried inside her mind. She didn't want to miss a single word. Impressed with her insight and straightforwardness, Anita recalled abuelas words:

> Because I worked from sunup to sundown as a fieldhand for years, my face was creased and lined before I was thirty! My children stayed by my side, as we crisscrossed the United States. We were migrant workers during awfully hard times. The farmers who hired us for the harvest didn't give us shelter worthy of human beings. The living quarters had no indoor bathrooms or running water—they were not even suitable for animals.

With the desire to understand how the family found themselves there, Anita asked "How did you end up in Michigan?" Abuela explained,

> We would have never ended up in Michigan if we had not been recruited to harvest sugar beets. Los Anglos agricultores wanted us because they paid us mere centavos! Sí. They took advantage of us. We had no choice. We needed money to survive and prosper.

Much was going on inside Anita's mind, as abuela shared the life she had lived, especially when her husband abandoned the family. However, that would not be the limit of her oppression.

In the United States, abuela spoke about experiencing countless denigrations. She elaborated: "In the United States we were referred to as migrants. I always thought it strange that people from Europe were called immigrants. ¿Por qué?"

She asked Anita, looking her in the eyes. She waited, expecting an answer. Anita had no response. She had never asked herself that question or wondered about it. Still, the conversation continued,

> Why aren't Mexicans called immigrants? We did not come here to move from place to place following the crops. Manuel was a bookkeeper. But I think one reason they did not hire him was that he was prieto dark skinned y lo discriminaban. Still, he could've found work.

Anita concluded that things had been difficult when Manuel didn't work. As abuelita tells the story, the times became more unbearable during that period which historians called the Great Depression—a time Maria Antonia named the gran devastación because of the damage it caused countless families. This was a time in history that many people never forgot.

The way abuela saw it, the years 1929 through 1936 left an indelible mark on her, prompting an impassioned lecture about never having compromised her moral values. She kept her dignity as she earned income to feed her children throughout these years of hardship. Abuela emphasized,

> I was young then, but I never relinquished my dignity. Nor did I bring shame to my family by working in bars or using my body as a means of making money. My religion taught me that my body was not intended to be handed over to a man, to overcome poverty.

Maria Antonia proudly told Ana to focus on her pride and commitment to herself. Then she raised her fist in the air, saying, "instead of selling my body or myself, I created an image that emphasized my circumstances." She detailed:

> I tied an old scarf around my head to increase the likelihood that people would think I was old. Then I bought a little red wagon and sold fruits and vegetables or grocery surplus thrown out at the supermarkets. To earn money to feed my children, I vended what seemed like a great bounty on Dallas streets, instead of selling myself.

She proudly recalled putting on her pantaloons, como las meras mujeres. And, like real women, I went to work as a roving grocer. This was how she kept her dignity, to ensure her children didn't starve. For emphasis abuela repeated, "¡Como las meras mujeres!" Like strong women, this experience undoubtedly filled her with impenetrable strength.

From abuela, Anita found out that, "it was through the generosity of Mexican-owned grocers and larger chains such as Atlantic & Pacific (A&P) and Safeway that I was able to pick through produce and canned goods thrown away daily." She would hoist the goods into her red wagon and for a dime she'd sell them to strangers and neighbors. She was proud about all she did to keep her family fed, to stay together. She added, "Even today, I'm not ashamed to say what I did to make sure we survived. Being resourceful allowed me to retain my dignity." Indeed, personal dignity was Maria Antonia's badge of honor. Whether she found herself working as a seamstress, a milliner, a dishwasher, a migrant or whatever, she held her head up high.

She recalled that in 1930s Dallas, there was a district run by mainly Jewish businessmen. This was a source of work for newly arrived Mexican immigrants who became the backbone of millinery, dressmaking, food services, and other industries such as carpentry and construction in Dallas and across Texas. Abuela continued with the story:

> There was a park near Harry Hines called el parque de los judíos or the Jewish Park, because immigrant Jews fre-

quently gathered there. We could see them through the window while we were at work ... far away from there was a grocery store called Hernández, which had been there since 1918, where I sent my children to buy sweet bread, pan dulce, and other food supplies.

Abuela had many beautiful memories of Dallas, where Jeorge was born. Her two oldest, had first attended elementary and middle school in Dallas. Still, despite these happy recollections, there were the tough years, when work was so scarce in that city that the family fell into the pattern of seasonal migration.

Maria Antonia experienced the sting of backbreaking work as far away as Florida and the Midwest. But believing that nothing defined a man or woman more than a strong work ethic, Maria Antonia plunged into migrant work with her children in tow. Abuela took Anita's hand, telling her, "Anita, see these wrinkled, arthritic hands? If they could talk to you right now, they would tell you about our never-ending struggle to survive." Young inquisitive Ana, whom she had lovingly given her the endearment Anita, would shake her head enthusiastically to show abuelita that she had indeed understood.

Then pressing her vein enriched hands into her palms, Maria Antonia added, "These old, worn-out hands have been burned by the sun, and damaged by the scrapes of countless harvests. These hands tell the story of struggle and survival in the United States and during the bloody Mexican Revolution."

Anita knew that Maria Antonia had entered the Unites States in 1924. Also, that abuelita had played a pivotal role in her upbringing. One of seventeen grandchildren, she loved Maria Antonia as if she were her biological mother—and never forgot her lifelong generosity and kindness. "Abuelita," her granddaughter interjected.

I still remember sometimes you'd walk all the way to our house in Saginaw to bring us bags of oranges, apples, and snacks. When we saw you clutching those bags, we'd run toward you. You looked exhausted and I was glad when my mother got into her Buick and took you home.

22

Anita's adoration for abuelita began at the age of six, when Maria Antonia sat in a rocking chair knitting hats for their cold Michigan winters. She'd sit on the floor beside her, warmed by her affection. Mesmerized by the firsthand accounts of Mexico's horrific peasant rebellion, Anita never failed to ask her for a story.

In Spanish, abuela told Anita,

> I've heard some people say they would like to return to the good old days. But I don't think those were good old days, especially not in Mexico. There were no modern conveniences, and during the revolutionary battles, times were much worse.

TODAY, SITTING IN her newly imposed wheelchair and sporting a new cropped haircut, Maria Antonia did not look her one-hundred-and-four years. Unlike her daughter, she had never worn lipstick. So, her thin, tiny lips remained red as raspberries. She had never applied face creams to retain her youth or plucked her eyebrows or used mascara on her lashes. "I have aged as God has intended," Maria Antonia told her audience. Yet, no one could confirm her age.

Her oldest son, Paco, came the closest to finding out what year she was born when he visited Muzquiz, his birthplace, after serving in World War II and Korea. At Santa Rosa de Lima parish where he and Minerva were baptized, Paco found their mother's baptismal records, and, for the first time, he saw her baptismal dates but not the date of her birth.

Paco, who had inherited his father's Indian heritage, with his dark skin, wide face, and high cheek bones, was surprised to see a date on the document. It showed Maria Antonia was much older than any of them had ever imagined—this would be conversations that often surfaced amongst them.

On a visit to Michigan from his home in Illinois, Paco asked his siblings. "Remember how we never knew how old our mother really was? Well, I found out she's a lot older than we thought. She was born on a ranch and baptized about a year later, her baptism document does not show her birth—there's no official record of her age."

Even so, they found out that she was born years before the Mexican Revolution. When Maria Antonia applied for Social Security, she gave 1901 as the year of her birth.

Maria Antonia's life appeared to be cloaked in mystery. It was not so much her age that amazed everyone, it was her health. What most astonished everyone was her memory. Her precise questions reflected her thinking. Although she had not seen Hilda Zonlak for nearly thirty years, she had not forgotten the many years in Michigan working and helping Hilda's parents. Gloria and Jeorge Castañeda raised her and her six siblings. Glad to see her after such a long absence, Maria Antonia approached Hilda and asked.

"Do you remember when I used to get you ready for school?"

"Sí." She replied, followed by the clarification that she didn't understand Spanish.

With a puzzled look, Maria Antonia tried again.

"Don't tell me you don't remember when I used to comb your long hair before sending you out the door?"

Despite her granddaughter's bewilderment, Maria Antonia continued.

Hilda's silence and blank stare made abuela realize it was useless to address her in Spanish. Almost as if making an excuse for her, abuela looked at Ana and uttered.

"Hilda was still a child when I moved to Texas with Minerva. I did not raise her as I did the older children—you, Mercedes, and Martha."

One of Minerva's five daughters, Ana was the only granddaughter who spoke, wrote, and read Spanish. From the moment she was born, she would forever become Anita, what Maria Antonia called her. While this made her feel special, abuela never showed more love for her than any of the other grandchildren. Nonetheless, she had a knack for making each grandchild feel truly loved.

During this visit, Hilda was shocked to hear that her aunt Minerva had abandoned her grandmother. And, while she had always heard stories about her eccentric aunt, she had respect for

Minerva. Thus, she withheld judgment even while mother and daughter argued about Maria Antonia's Texas home.

When Maria Antonia lived with them, Hilda's parents spoke Spanish, but when she and her daughter moved to Texas, her sisters and only brother stopped speaking Spanish. She was ten years old when their grandmother moved away. That's when the whole family reverted to English only.

Hilda Zonlak had married a Polish American and had grown children of her own. The one regret she had was not having maintained the language. She tried communicating in "Spanglish" but seemed embarrassed. So rather than incite Maria Antonia's ire, she spoke English and simply used hand-gestures when addressing her grandmother.

"You look beautiful with your new hairstyle, abuelita."

Using body language, she continued giving her instructions.

"Now, the nurse is going to take your temperature and check your blood pressure, because this is an exciting day."

Maria Antonia shook her head as if she understood. But nobody knew for sure.

That abuela had never learned to speak, read, or write English was a mystery to those outside her family. By contrast, she could not understand why, except for Anita, her grandchildren and her great-grandchildren were not verbal and literate in Spanish. Yet, when asked why she had never learned to speak English. Abuela said,

> Many people ask me why I didn't learn English. In the United States we were often segregated. Even though we worked and lived among the bolillos—what we called Anglos—they didn't befriend us. People think only Negroes were discriminated against and segregated, but we were treated just like them.

She added, "The United States is not the country I entered. We migrated because they wanted Mexicans—we are hard-working people. So, we left a country torn by war. The most important thing is that we survived."

To gauge her descendants' reactions, Maria Antonia offered, "I don't regret coming here, my grandchildren and great-grandchildren are reaping the rewards. And speaking broken English never stopped me from working and earning money." For abuela, the struggle was beyond that of language.

IN THE 1940S, Maria Antonia persuaded her youngest son, Beto, to leave Dallas for Michigan, where agricultural jobs were plentiful. Her daughter's first husband, Manuel López, was in the U.S. Army stationed overseas. Not wanting to be alone, her only daughter—Minerva—agreed to join them.

Talk and rumors of an ensuing worldwide war dominated local radio stations. All were tuned in to hear the updates.

Although Maria Antonia's two oldest sons, Paco and Jeorge were of age for the mandatory draft, the two brothers joined the US Army because they felt it was their patriotic duty to serve.

Hilda recalled abuela had lived with her family for many years. Her father, Jeorge, had been a paratrooper in the U. S. Army. He invited veterans of the same war over to visit and between shots of tequila, they traded war stories. After a few shots, they'd compare wounds from their harrowing experiences.

Maria Antonia's oldest son, Paco, was the first to enlist in the U.S. Army during World War II. He was a permanent resident who received a green card as a child, so he was accepted. Trained as a paratrooper, his motive was to defend the nation, not to earn citizenship.

In 2003, The University of Texas School of Journalism in Austin created a broadsheet newspaper focused on the contributions of Mexican America men and women during World War II. Titled "Narratives," the paper included Jeorge. He had served in the 187th Airborne Regimental Combat Team. Although wounded in action, Jeorge was reassigned after recovering from his injuries. At the hospital, when the commanding general learned of his bravery in the face of danger, the general assigned him to a special mission involving the rescue of American soldiers behind enemy lines. He single-handedly completed the charge to the great satisfaction of his superiors. Jeorge recalled the general's visit.

"When I was wounded and taken to the hospital, I thought that was the end of the war, for me. But I was selected for that special mission," Jeorge told a reporter, who interviewed him when he was seventy-seven and disabled from a stroke and heart attack. During the interview, featuring unsung Hispanic heroes and war veterans, Jeorge said that the only thing that saved him was his mother's prayers. In addition to fervently praying for her sons' safe return, she sent them letters. Often, she persuaded family members or friends to write these. Illiteracy was a major consternation for Maria Antonia. However, to anyone who listened she would often chastise Mexico.

> There, not everyone had the opportunity to read and write. Small towns like Muzquiz did not always have teachers. We went to school when we could. I learned to write my name, but I needed help to write my sons. When a family member wasn't around, a friend would help.

Months before her one-hundred-and-third birthday. A Texas judge would authorize abuela's transfer to Michigan, contingent on a family member serving as official guardian. Hilda had come to visit abuela after the Texas Department of Family and Protective Services forced Maria Antonia out of her home.

When abuela was transported to Michigan, Hilda, a stay-at-home mother, took on the time-consuming requirements of legal guardianship. With moral support from the immediate family, Hilda accepted the charge and focused on abuela's care, as no relative's home was suitable or available for that. All Maria Antonia's children were now frail and elderly.

BECAUSE PROFESSIONAL home health care was too expensive, the family learned to rely on Hilda, as various health conditions emerged among the older generation. While Jeorge was Maria Antonia's pride and joy, he was unable to provide care in his own home. Gloria, his seventy-five-year-old wife, who cared for Jeorge since his health problems arose, could not add to her load. Maria Antonia's youngest son, Beto, had a massive heart attack at seventy. Mary, his seventy-four-year-old wife, had diabetes—a condition she had ignored until she was hospitalized. Among them other health concerns surfaced. So, none of their family members were able open their home. Also, Minerva had been diagnosed with diabetes, a disease she had refused to acknowledge, until she nearly slipped into a coma. After she recovered, Minerva returned to Michigan, leaving the Texas home she'd shared for decades with her mother.

Gina, one of two daughters from Minerva's third marriage, took her in when she could no longer tolerate her mother. Also, the renters often threatened to call social services about the unruly adopted child she was raising. The five-year-old boy displayed aggressive behavior, hitting Maria Antonia in the face with a toy when he pleased.

When Maria Antonia agreed with the renters, Minerva became enraged. However, no one in the family ever imagined Minerva would abandon her ninety-eight-year-old mother. It was then that she left Maria Antonia in her dilapidated San Antonio home. The Texas Department of Family and Protective Services was called for help but only responded when Minerva left. To this day it's still unclear whether Maria Antonia was forced from her home because of the State's fear of being sued by the family. Anita, Hilda and her brother, George Jr., teamed up to persuade the Bexar County Family Court judge to release Maria Antonia to their care.

Three weeks after Maria Antonia had been strapped to a gurney, taken to a hospital, and transferred to a deplorable nursing home, they took on the Texas court system. Attorney fees were paid by her son, Jeorge. The judge ruled in their favor and Maria Antonia could be transported to a Michigan nursing home, so long as the facility offered 24-seven care. Also, the judge stated unequivocally that Maria Antonia would transfer to Michigan, if, and only if, a family member consented to this type of nursing home.

Visibly stressed by the order, Hilda swore under oath that she would comply. In Frankenmuth, Michigan, Hilda found two nursing homes that met the criteria. She selected the one with an excellent reputation—it had a medical staff to deal with the urgent care needs of its fifty residents. The only drawback was that no one spoke Spanish, so Maria Antonia spent hours in silence until a family member came to visit.

During this time, Maria Antonia's focus of conversation was about the home she was forced to leave. She longed to find out what happened to it. She yearned to return to that place she purchased in 1976—when she bought that San Antonio home—a year after they arrived. The realtor was speechless, when her daughter translated that Maria Antonia proposed $11,000 cash for the condemned house listed at $12,000.

When the offer was accepted, they rejoiced over the turn-of-the century two-story seedy southside house, which had rotted wood floors and no insulation. The house had been an eyesore, prompting the city of San Antonio to post a "this property is condemned" sign. At that time in the city's history, the southside of town was blighted. Residents of the community were mainly poor, working-class Mexicans.

Regardless of the condition of her house, Maria Antonia felt at home because everyone spoke Spanish. However, the southside of San Antonio was the space that contained the most elegant, palatial homes in the state. Built by wealthy German settlers and situated only a few blocks away from Maria Antonia's house, this was the part of town where all but one historic Spanish mission was situated. Even so, the city had neglected its southside in favor of other areas, thus making it affordable for poor Mexicans and some born in the United States who bought or rented wood-framed homes. Most houses needed a new roof, a fresh coat of paint, and basic modern conveniences. However, to Maria Antonia the house was a palace. It was her palace. When her sons or a family member called, she proudly told them she bought a house with cash. With her own money, and, most importantly, she took pride in the security of knowing that for the third time in her life, she was a homeowner. Maria Antonia proclaimed:

> Aquí estamos y ahora sí nos vamos a quedar. Minerva y yo no tenemos que rendir cuentas a nadie. ¡De aquí al cielo hijo! We're here to stay! Minerva and I are not beholden to anyone, she told her son Jeorge on that telephone call announcing the purchase—now, from here to heaven.

When Maria Antonia's sons and the rest of the family heard she bought a house, and that mother and daughter would live together, they wobbled their collective heads in disbelief. The two of them had never seen eye-to-eye on anything. Relatives predicted the two would continue arguing and bickering as they always had.

Marriage would be the only way she could escape from her mother, and like Maria Antonia, Minerva's first marriage was officiated at the same age as Maria Antonia—at seventeen.

Minerva forever spoke about finding ways to escape her mother. And, once again, she'd be under her roof.

As all this was happening in Texas, Anita relocated to Dallas with her husband, Vicente Mas, as soon as he graduated from a Michigan university. His first professional job was in the computer industry. After buying their first home, determined to make her way toward a BA in English literature, Anita enrolled in a nearby community college. It was not only a coincidence that her mother and grandmother moved to Texas—it was serendipitous as she would see her closest family members which would enable her to chronicle Maria Antonia's history and that of the Menchaca-Castañeda family.

Anita did not waste time. She soon began asking abuela interminable questions in Spanish, as Anita told her,

> I want to write about how you came to the United States. I want to tell your story so that other Mexican immigrants may be inspired by it. Did you know that more than a million Mexicans crossed into the United States during and after the revolution?

Abuela did not hesitate to answer Anita's questions. As if to support the knowledge her granddaughter brought into the conversation, abuela said:

> When your grandfather and I crossed the border, we saw hundreds of people crossing alongside us. We all wanted a better life with more opportunities. We wanted to find work and make a way for our children to have a life free of war and poverty and changing governments like those in Mexico.

Those talks were detailed in Anita's journal, as she worked part time and tended to her own two children, while completing a college degree. Through her formal education, Anita finally had time to think about the stories her grandmother told her as a child.

On frequent visits from Dallas to San Antonio, long before her mother abandoned Maria Antonia, Anita eagerly engaged her grandmother in lengthy conversations about her upbringing and her departure from Mexico.

During those times she listened intently with pen in hand, jotting down specific incidents. More curious than anxious to know what she'd written, Maria Antonia asked.

"Anita, mi alma. Pues, ¿Qué escribes?"

She hoped that abuela truly believed her when she said she found her life and her family's stories interesting. With that in mind, she told abuela, "Tu vida y tus historias son muy interesantes."

Still, abuela did not like being interviewed, not even by her granddaughter. Anyone who had tried probing her past quickly learned Maria Antonia had a knack for replying with her own rhetorical questions. For example, abuela told Anita about her recent experience with Texas agencies.

> Since I was taken from my home by force and brought to this nursing home in Michigan, many people have been asking me questions about my personal life. Why do they want to know about me? Why am I so interesting now? I never asked the government for a thing. I worked for

everything I had, including my three homes. And I always paid my property taxes.

Before returning to her former home state, Maria Antonia had never received so much attention. She had been poked and prodded more than at any time in her life. It was disconcerting to her. And it was not just because of her confinement to a nursing home. Their interest focused on her excellent physical and mental health.

This mystery, while a joy to her family, had prompted questions from doctors and nursing staff. Rosa, Hilda's sister, was a nurse at a Detroit hospital. When she told staffers about Maria Antonia, they urged Rosa to interview abuela to find out what she had done to live a long healthy life, even though Anita had long begun the queries.

Characteristically, Maria Antonia reacted with suspicion to any questions. She saw them as invasive and intruding into her personal life. The trust Maria Antonia had built over the years with Anita did not extend to the other grandchildren. When Anita realized that Maria Antonia felt threatened by anyone who tried to scrutinize or record her stories, Anita became a better listener. She developed more patience and learned to take mental notes, convinced that abuelita's life was worth writing about.

Over the years and through abuelita's stories, Anita memorized interesting incidents. Most of all she realized that because other grandchildren did not speak Spanish it was her duty and her mission to record her life. During those three years Maria Antonia spent in the Frankenmuth nursing home, abuelita continued to insist she had been railroaded. She often recounted how a Texas doctor had questioned her at the hospital emergency room trying to determine if she had dementia or Alzheimer's disease. To let Anita know how she felt, she repeated what she had already said in Spanish:

When they forced me into the San Antonio nursing home, I had done nothing! I had asked for nothing! I had paid my property taxes, my utilities, telephone bills. And I bought my own food. I never asked the government for anything.

While Maria Antonia's repetition could be misinterpreted, she reminded Anita that she had survived the Great Depression. Also, with four mouths to feed, and accustomed to hard times, Maria Antonia was never without cash or savings. She nearly saved every penny she had earned. There was never any excuse not to save at least a penny, she would tell anyone who listened or asked. As a child, Anita recalled that every Tuesday after school she went with her abuelita to the local bank. That was the day Maria Antonia collected her weekly paycheck from the bakery. She would deposit cash and then show her a tiny book in which the bank teller had recorded the amount deposited, explaining,

> Hija mia, my daughter, many people squander their money. They work all their lives and have nothing to show for their work. That's because they never made saving money a habit. When you grow up, always put money aside. Always save more than you spend, siempre!

For emphasis, Maria Antonia stressed, "If you learn to save your money, you will never be poor. You will never have to ask others for money when you need it. You will always be self-sufficient. If you save, you'll be able to help your family."

Maria Antonia called Franklin D. Roosevelt, her favorite American president, el viejito. Then she took Anita on a memory journey:

> I opened my first bank account when old man Roosevelt started programs to put people back to work during the Depression. He also started the Social Security program, which began by taking one dollar from all the workers.

Abuela was a good businesswoman. Since she had rented out the first floor of her Michigan home for years, abuela viewed renters as secondary sources of income. So, despite her San Antonio home's precarious inclination, it became a rooming house for a select group of people. In Texas authorities were shocked to learn that the limited English-speaking centenarian had rented out the first floor of her modest home since 1976. A monthly social security check and money from poor people did not prevent her from saving an impressive sum of money.

The tenancies of her homes became a way for her to remain independent for decades. Her inquilinos renters were mainly hard-working Mexicans. Some worked as hotel maids, waitresses, and school janitors. Knowing they earned a pittance of a salary filled her with compassion prompting her to charge monthly rent accordingly. She had to be solvent in her finances, since she never had learned to drive, didn't have a car, and could no longer walk upright, she had no choice but to stash her money away when her daughter left.

On her monthly visits, when she drove from Dallas to San Antonio, Anita was astonished to discover just how adamant Maria Antonia was about saving.

> Anita mia, now that you're here, I want you to do something. But you must do exactly as I say. Go to the living room and look in the dresser. Remove the third drawer. Behind the drawer remove a bundle of newspapers. Bring them here to me.

Anita brough the bundle to her and when Maria Antonia unfolded the newspapers, several 100-dollar bills went flying. Anita always felt like a child around her grandmother, and the day she saw money flying, she felt like Alice in Wonderland, and cried in absolute amazement.

> Abuelita! You must not save money this way. It is very dangerous to hide cash in the house. That can endanger you. Someone could break in here, too. You must let me take your money to the bank!

One of the things Anita most admired about abuelita was her uncanny ability to save. Anita wanted to be to be just like her. But seeing this amount of money flying high above made her fear for her grandmother's life.

Anita was taken aback when she found that her grandmother had saved an impressive amount of money since her last visit. The people she rented to were not people from whom anyone could profit. The renters were poor people who lived from paycheck to paycheck, and a meager paycheck at that. Sometime later, she found out some of the renters pawned watches, rings and other valuables they'd acquired to pay for their rent. Most had menial jobs or they had no job at all, which meant they received food stamps through federal programs or assistance from local non-profit agencies.

Most of her inquilinos, however, were desperate hardworking Mexicans who had entered the country without government-sanctioned documentation. Abuela empathized with them because she too had come as an immigrant and like them worked for peanuts. Defiantly, abuelita told Anita,

> How can I turn them away? They are newcomers without a place to live. I was also an immigrant. Before we entered the United States, I opened a taco cafe on the Laredo border to help your grandfather make ends meet. When he left me, nobody took pity on me and my children. I quickly learned that as a family we all had to work to survive.

Anita was told by her mother Minerva, that abuela once had a thriving café in Nuevo Laredo. With a profound sense of duty to her "semejantes," her human peers, abuela served free hot coffee and a variety of pan dulces—sweetbread—to prisoners on a chain gang.

From family members, her grandchildren had heard many examples of abuela's generosity and kindness. While growing up, despite their fatherless home, her children never lacked for anything. Above all, Maria Antonia was loyal to her children. Minerva, who would forever refer to her mother as Toña, recalled a story about her determination to be self-sufficient, by the ways Maria Antonia cared for them. Minerva provided an example:

> Toña bought me seven dresses, one for each day of the week. She would handwash them and iron them each weekend. She didn't want me to ever go to school in wrinkled clothes, scraggly hair, and unkempt.

On a rare occasion, when Minerva spoke highly about her mother, she surprised her daughters with an unexpected comment:

> When I went to school I was so well dressed and groomed that I was never offered a free lunch like the other children. Toña made sure my long hair was combed. She even put a big bow in my hair.

Sadly, Maria Antonia was trapped in a nursing home, where she marked time reflecting on her lengthy life with family members. Those with whom she conversed noted that she was even more intent on reaffirming her decision to leave Mexico with her husband, his children, and their two children in tow. Maria Antonia repeated the stories to demonstrate her ability to recall, as she shared memories of her life. She said,

> Between the revolution and the desperate times, we lived in Mexico afterward, I dreamed of leaving and never returning. That's why when my husband and I entered the United States, I knew I was here to stay. All I had was a fourth-grade education, but I came with a strong desire to rise above that. When Manuel and I crossed the border, we had just been married five years. I didn't know he was a man who didn't worry about getting ahead. He was content with a low paying job or no job at all. He was the opposite of me. I always believed in working hard to get ahead.

Her modest upbringing did not prepare her to become a migrant worker, earning meager wages from picking cotton in tiny towns across Texas. She had envisioned staying at home and raising her children. She was not prepared for seasonal backbreaking work gathering corn, wheat, and all manner of fruits and vegetables, following the northeast migrant trail in the United States.

Because of her life circumstances, instead of feeling hatred, anger or bitterness, hard times had engendered in her a resolve that was as impenetrable as steel. Woeful and wretched were not words anyone could ever use to describe abuelita. Maria Antonia knew that action was the only way to deal with despair. She never sat around waiting for something to happen. If something needed to be done, especially if it involved survival, she took the bull by the horns.

A philosophy of survival gave abuelita the strength she needed. Foundational to her philosophy was the belief that we are those whom we emanate from and strength comes from within. We inherit family traits, good or bad. Todo se hereda, everything is inherited. When she tried to understand her only daughter, abuela would often say, "La sangre hace su deber, the blood is true to itself," as she explored the similarities.

> Minerva isn't at all like me. She took after Manuel in several ways. She loves to read and hates backbreaking migratory work. She has never worried about what others may say if she does not follow society's norms. But I don't think you can go through life breaking rules and traditions.

Contrary to Minerva, Maria Atonia considered herself a poor simple person who didn't have the opportunity to get a good education. She didn't like people who bragged. She had little patience with those who tried to make her or her children feel inferior.

Through their conversations, Anita recognized that her grandmother had grown up poor and in a war-torn country with a bleak future. Still, she admired the ways in which intelligence, resourcefulness, and shrewdness enabled her to rise above insurmountable challenges. Abuelita would often say,

> Many people who have come here are doing well now. They suffered during the revolution, as we did. Instead of embracing us because we went through the same horrors, since acquiring businesses and money, they turn their noses up and away. I do not admire such behavior, and I've taught my children not to become snobs.

Unfortunately, due to Minerva's thirst for independence and desire to be of a higher social status, abuela's examples and her teachings fell on deaf ears. Minerva often dressed in such a glamorous fashion that she was criticized by the Mexican female peers of the tiny Michigan town. As she got ready to attend a dance, Minerva did not fear going against her mother.

> I'm not like the other Mexican girls who wear those ugly black-and-white saddle shoes, white ankle socks, and long wool skirts to go to a dance. I know how to dress properly, and those girls who do not are jealous of me.

While growing up in Dallas, Minerva had been introduced to haute couture. That is why she did not fit in when the family moved to a small Michigan town. There, most of the time, she wore two-piece suits, hosiery and heels. When she went dancing, however her dresses looked like those found in fashion magazines. To complement her wardrobe, her two-inch high-heeled shoes always matched her dresses, which were every color but black. Her long, brown hair was put up in a sexy chignon a la Grace Kelly. The sleek, cat-like way she walked attracted young men and sparked envy among competitive young local women. When abuelita got after her, Minerva would add,

> I'm not like anyone else. And I don't care what they say about me. I know the women in this town are just jealous because I'm free! I'm free of Manuel now, and Jesús is no longer in my life. So, I can date, go to dances and live my life.

Abuela recognized Minerva's heartlessness and the ways in which she took advantage of her generosity and she was concerned for her grandchildren. She recalled,

> Desde luego, como yo siempre fui su niñera. Of course, because I was always her babysitter. Así se divertía y pudo encontrar su tercer marido. That was the way she had a blast and snared her third husband. Sadly, Minerva forgot she was the mother of three beautiful daughters.

In-between worlds of poverty and opulence, Maria Antonia recognized that she lived in a world where inequality was ever-present.

Both Mexico and the United States had in common the traps of inequality and exploitation she confronted.

IN 1900, during Porfirio Diaz's fourth consecutive term, the population of Mexico had swelled to more than 15 million. More than a third of the population, however, worked as peones on fewer than 800 haciendas that were owned by more than half of Mexico, and those who owned the haciendas were reaping most of the riches. The nation was predominantly Indigenous, made up of several nations, including but not limited to Coahuiltecos, Kickapoos, and Huachichiles, among others. They held tightly to their ancient customs, norms, and language. Of course, many were mestizos, of mixed Spanish and Indigenous heritage.

Institutional discrimination and neglect made it easier for government officials to circumvent basic human necessities. Viewed as uneducated and unworthy of being landowners, most Mexicans didn't own land and were subservient in their own homeland. Abject poverty and social injustices prevailed, relegating Indigenous people into a caste system in which el patrón was king. Still, Independence from Spain in 1821 did not end racial and class injustices. By 1910, the Mexican Revolution erupted like a volcano.

It is thought that Maria Antonia was born in 1901, nine years before Mexicans rose up and demanded equal rights, social justice, and ownership of the land. A local midwife, Juana Vega, delivered abuelita on that hot summer night. It was not uncommon for women to give birth at home. Her father, Roque Menchaca, lost his wife and he became a young widower when Maria Antonia was three. He was left with her as his only child, to raise on his modest ranch, which was located near Muzquiz, in the state of Coahuila, in northern Mexico.

With the death of his wife, Roque Menchaca had no choice but to ask Juana Vega to help him bring up Maria Antonia in her infancy. Although she had a family in another town near Muzquiz,

Juana agreed to help Roque Menchaca for an indefinite time in exchange for food, lodging, and a nominal fee.

Maria Antonia spoke lovingly and fondly of her father. She said he was six feet three inches tall, and he was a blue-eyed and red-headed man. Later, Minerva would spread the erroneous conclusion that her maternal grandfather was Irish. The absence of any birth or baptismal records of an Irish surname in Mexico to substantiate the claim went unnoticed by most family members. Consequently, what originally was a Spanish-Basque ancestral physical trait remained a lifelong imaginary Irish illusion.

From Mexicans who had traveled to the United States, Maria Antonia had heard conversations about the great misconceptions gringos had about Mexicans. The vast majority did not realize many Mexicans were of mixed heritage, and that they had ancestry other than Indian. In fact, they didn't understand the conquistadores hailed from diverse regions of Spain, especially the Basque area known as País Vasco.

Moreover, Hollywood movies perpetuated the image of Mexicans dressed in white shirts, white cotton pants, and a large hat sombrero made of straw. In the United States, this image was firmly implanted in the minds of Anglos and other non-Mexicans.

Waves of immigrants into the United States had erased the proper spelling of Spanish surnames and their accentuation. Mexican families were lucky if their own family members handed down the bequest of their ancestry, thus losing a legacy rich in language, culture, and heritage. Maria Antonia knew who she was.

> From the time I was a child, I knew who I was. My father and my two aunts who raised me always talked about our Spanish roots. They even taught me that the term "Gachupin" was a common derogatory word used to express disdain for Spanish landowners.

Most Anglos knew little about Mexico's history. Although more than half of the United States once belonged to Mexico, they didn't know or learn that nation was made up of many ethnic groups. Sephardic Jews and a host of descendants originally from Ireland, Asia, Germany and other countries called Mexico home. Abuela said,

> What estadounidenses or people of the United States never understood was that those who crossed the border after the Mexican Revolution were escaping unending warfare. Those who had survived economically believed democracy was an ideal that would never work in Mexico.

We often heard that, when abuela entered the United States, she often was mistaken for a European immigrant because of her physical appearance. With alabaster skin and her neck and arms dotted with strawberry-colored birthmarks, abuelita's auburn hair and hazel eyes challenged the Mexican stereotype of brown skin and black hair and eyes. Anglo Americans attributed her ancestry to Ireland.

"You can't be from Mexico. You don't look Mexican," many exclaimed upon discovering her background. Still, Maria Antonia never lost her sense of identity. Her father had made her keenly aware of her Spanish-Basque heritage, as well as her "mestiza" identity, because of her mother's Indigenous heritage.

Maria Antonia said her father's marriage to an Indian woman was never frowned upon by his family. At the time, prejudice dictated a man's duty to retain his "purity of blood." This dominant norm prevailed even after Mexico's independence. Still, Roque Menchaca never felt alienated by his family, given the traditions and views that permeated amongst them.

Maria Antonia grew up internalizing institutional prejudices. She also said, her father told her that he had been disinherited. Forty years later, Anita would find that in Spain it was a custom for only the first born to inherit family property. The remaining siblings were left with no choice but to emigrate to other countries. As a result, many who left Mexico have Spanish Basque ancestry.

It was not as if the Menchaca clan had royal blood. Indeed, Spain's royal family would not be among those who left for the Americas. Rather, according to Maria Antonia, retaining "purity of blood" was a family's duty to not mix. This duty was worth its weight in gold, and commanded respect, ensuring family genealogy.

Fully accepting that she was mestiza, Maria Antonia had always viewed her father's disinherited status as an injustice. This unjust tradition had inspired her lifelong empathy toward the Indian population of Mexico. Sympathy for the long-suffering Indigenous Mexicans may have been another reason she married Manuel Castañeda, a Coahuilteco Indian, who had grown up in Coahuila.

It is a historic fact that Spain and Mexico recognized the offspring of a Spaniard and an Indian as mestizos. After the arrival of Hernán Cortez, the Spanish called this merger el mestizaje. But it is equally factual that acceptance was another story. Abuelita recognized that, "mis hijos reflejan la raza india y española. My children reflect both Indian and Spanish blood. Al fin y al cabo, el indio es la raza más pura. After all, the Indian race is the purest of races," Maria Antonia said, when recalling her two sons' experiences with racial discrimination in the United States. Aware of the pervasive inhumanity expressed toward those who were decreed as inferior, at a young age, Maria Antonia had noticed the harsh treatment of mestizos by wealthy landowners called hacendados. Later, she learned the Menchaca clan had legal title allowing them to own property. Many Mexicans didn't have property rights at that time.

From birth until the age of nine, Maria Antonia lived with her hard-working, benevolent father. He had grown to depend on Juana Vega to help nurse and nurture Maria Antonia. She left her own family for a time to help raise her, since she had grown up without her mother. Maria Antonia was surrounded by love and care. Her father played his violin when he was not tending to his cattle. It was Maria Antonia's first introduction to music. She loved listening to Roque's classical repertoire, which included traditional Spanish jotas, paso dobles, and coplas. Thanks to his influence, Maria Antonia learned to sing the lyrics.

Life on the isolated ranch was challenging, if not downright daunting. Nonetheless, Maria Antonia found horseback riding gave her self-confidence and independence. For this very reason she quickly became the youngest and most astute equestrian in Coahuila.

Her father lovingly called his only daughter, "Toñita," rather than use her given name. When her father watched her compete with older male equestrians, he was filled with pride. Her ruggedness became the foundation from which she would overcome life's challenges. Soon, he agonized over a decision that would dramatically change both their lives, still he approached his daughter.

"Toñita, you're growing like a wild nopal, and I have not yet told you the story of how, when, and why my family arrived in Mexico, as I need to make a decision that involves your future." Roque Menchaca paused and said, pointing to a huge trunk stored under his iron bed,

> First, I need to tell you about that old trunk, the one I keep under my bed. It contains precious remnants of my heritage. My sisters and brothers agreed to let me keep it when our parents died. The trunk contains proof they arrived in Mexico in the 1860s.

Maria Antonia looked with great curiosity at the enormous trunk he kept locked away under the bed in which she was born. Her mother had died in that bed. All she knew about the trunk or el baúl was that it contained a Bible and important legal documents he cherished. He seldom spoke about his siblings, Melecio, Francisco, Gilberto, Fulgencio, Teofela, and Enriqueta. Since she had grown up on the ranch, Maria Antonia had never met any of them. That is why she listened intently when her father decided to recount a bit of his family's history. Her father began,

> When my parents arrived here, Mexico was said to be a country filled with gold and silver. A land of new opportunities. They were young and willing to work hard despite the great risk of financial disaster. So, they settled near Muzquiz when the silver mines were in their glory.

Roque's parents related to him the conditions under which they had left. Before Spain became a country, it consisted of various kingdoms. Roque Menchaca's original Basque name was spelled Roke Mentxaka, in the native Basque language of Eusquera. He detailed,

43

While we know our Spanish-Basque heritage, we're proud Mexicans because we were born here. My brothers in Muzquiz are business owners. But I wanted to own land so I could farm it. My two sisters are truly refined and industrious women. They are spinsters who own a two-story house in town. They sell their handmade goods to locals, and they received help from my brothers.

Entranced by her father's blue eyes, Maria Antonia listened. He talked about the family history and the relatives she didn't know. Physically aged beyond his forty years, Roque Menchaca put his hands gently on Maria Antonia and told her she was going to live with his sisters. He said, bracing himself for her predictable protest,

I have written to Teofela and Enriqueta. And they have agreed that you should live with them in the city. They will make sure you grow up to be a fine and proper young lady. They will be sure you marry someone who will take good care of you.

A rambunctious child, she was old enough to question how she would fit into the new family her father was describing. She adored her father and felt his love had kept her from feeling the loss of her mother. It had never occurred to her that she would leave him, the ranch, and her horse. She protested, "But papa, why do I have to go to Muzquiz?" Maria Antonia cried, telling her father, "I love living here with you, and I love my Pedro. I don't know Aunt Teofela and Aunt Enriqueta. I don't care that they are well bred and live in a beautiful house on the outskirts of town."

Headstrong Maria Antonia didn't win her battle to stay in the ranch. Roque Menchaca did not relent. He promised to care for Pedro, telling her he would visit as often as possible. Although Roque loved Maria Antonia more than life itself, in May of 1910, he decided that she was better off being brought up by his sisters.

Roque had heard rumblings about political unrest and the imminent threat of an uprising. These stirrings led him to believe his ranch and his daughter would be at risk, if government soldiers began crushing a peon revolt, or whether being caught in the middle by rampaging revolutionaries who were equally dangerous. Roque Menchaca was a man of few words. He thought about the possibility of keeping Maria Antonia in hiding nearby. But if he did that, he would expose her to other dangers from wild animals who roamed the vast lands.

After considerable soul searching and a heavy heart, Roque packed Maria Antonia's clothes and resolved to deliver her to the home of his sisters. Her tears and pleas about her impending tenth birthday were to no avail. He insisted she could celebrate it in Muzquiz. Unfortunately, their fate was sealed.

Alarming news filled the pages of a local newspaper owned by Melecio Menchaca, Roque's brother. News accounts talked about the large number of men who had left their backbreaking menial farm work to join Francisco "Pancho" Villa, a former laborer who had become a revolutionary.

Lack of communication had insulated Maria Antonia and her father from the impending revolt. The peasants viewed President Porfirio Diaz as a dictator. Outrage over his disregard for the poor raged amongst them. Upper class Mexicans with large estates flourished, while U.S. presidents and politicians favorably viewed Diaz during the many years he was in power.

Through those years, Diaz had invited Americans, Germans, and others, to invest in Mexico, and foreigners ended up owning Mexico. To Diaz, the mistreatment of Mexican laborers was inconsequential. Brutality, low wages, and racial discrimination toward Mexicans was viewed as "collateral damage" by Diaz and his cronies. He saw it as excusable in his quest to modernize Mexico.

Roque Menchaca was not aware of the number of peasants from Morelos who joined Emiliano Zapata and heeded his battle cry of "Tierra y Libertad." In 1910, Francisco I. Madero was regarded by many as an ideal replacement to Porfirio Diaz. But his faithful supporters, "Maderistas," feared for his life. Madero forged ahead criticizing the government and writing about his views in a book.

Roque Menchaca did not subscribe to any newspapers. Consequently, he was unaware of Madero's views on democracy which included giving Mexicans the right to a legitimate vote. He never heard of Madero's arrest by Diaz's operatives. Later, Roque learned that upon his release from jail Madero had fled to San Antonio, Texas.

Aside from his lack of knowledge concerning Mexican politics, Roque Menchaca didn't know that under the Porfiriato Mexico was not a democracy. He didn't realize that his brother Melecio Menchaca could be arrested for printing the truth. Because under Díaz, the press was restricted and repressed, regardless of what other nations thought of Mexico.

In the winter of 1908, Diaz agreed to do an interview with a United States magazine. He said that he would not resign until there was another man dignified enough to fill his shoes. To the dismay of most Mexicans, the story praised Diaz as the greatest Mexican of all time. Meanwhile, William Howard Taft, the twenty-ninth president of the United States had been elected to office in 1909. His administration had heard about how Mexico's dictator had doggedly held on to power. His administration had been willing to tolerate the alarming news about Díaz iron-fisted hold on his country. Nevertheless, by the fall of 1910, Taft's administration began to distrust Diaz. Mexican journalists got the warning that Diaz was bent on controlling the media. Aware of the simmering unrest, Taft began conversations with Madero, while he was living in exile in San Antonio.

A desire to see its neighbor become a bonafide democracy with a constitution that would offer its citizenry the right to vote unencumbered by physical threats was one of several reasons Taft supported Madero, according to historical accounts.

Unfortunately for poor, powerless and disenfranchised Mexicans of modest means, no part of Mexico would be spared from an imminent blood bath; a blood bath that would leave at least one million Mexicans dead in its wake. Those left standing were the politicians who would again betray the people of Mexico in their quest for personal wealth and power.

Roque Menchaca did not communicate often enough with his family in Muzquiz to know the extent of the ensuing malaise. He lived entrenched in his ranch, where Maria Antonia had been raised on goat's milk. Fieldhands and farm laborers were unreliable, so he did much of the work.

Teofela and Enriqueta Menchaca spent the day cooking, sewing, and caring for their extensive garden. Francisco Menchaca, a bachelor searching for a wife, enjoyed their home cooked meals. His furniture-making business kept him busy. Gilberto Menchaca had a grocery store while his brother Fulgencio Menchaca owned a bar. With revolution looming, he was sure they'd have to go out of business.

A few days before Roque Menchaca was to take Maria Antonia into Muzquiz, he heard hoofs pounding in the distance. The rapid fire-pounding sounds sent a chill up his spine. Sweating like never before. He sprang from the fence he had been repairing, shouting "Toñita, ¿Dónde estas?"

She was near the waterfall, where she had promised to work with Pedro to ensure that he no longer feared crossing the stream. While coaxing Pedro along, he came galloping up on his own horse yelling at her to head home. She noted the urgency in his voice, for he never raised his voice at her.

While Maria Antonia understood the unusual urgency, something deep inside told her not to ask why, but to obey him. The two rushed back to their modest house in time to tie up their horses and hide underneath the house. Pulsating sounds of approaching horses grew louder.

As Maria Antonia and her father cowered in the crawl space beneath the front porch, they heard one man say to the mustachioed bandolero, "Oye Nacho, ¡no hay nadie aquí!" Apparently, Nacho was the leader of the rifle-toting ragtag group. Still, he surveyed the exterior of the modest dwelling suspiciously.

Then Nacho, whose thick dark mustache made him look comical underneath his huge, broad-rimmed hat, shouted, "Yes. Indeed, there was someone in the house." Fear gripped Maria Antonia when she heard him insist someone was inside. Roque Menchaca cautioned in silence, putting his index finger to his lips. Father and daughter held tightly to one another breathing heavily in fear that the worst was still to come. They prayed and suffered in silence as they heard horses making noise all around.

"Salgan. Salgan," he barked. When his command went unanswered, the leader shouted: "¿Dónde está el jefe?" ¿Quién vive aquí?" Where is the boss? And Who lives here? Questions that fell on deaf ears angered him even more. Then the man the others called Nacho took his rifle and shot into the sky.

"Más vale que sean Villistas o verán como pagan," he barked, warning that whoever was hiding had better reveal themselves or else, clarifying that they better be Villistas, meaning in favor of Pancho Villa's División del Norte, or they would pay dearly.

Although fear gripped father and daughter, they sprang from beneath the porch.

"Sí. Sí. Somos Villistas. Somos Villistas," Roque Menchaca said, pleading with them not to harm his daughter. "Por favor, no dañen a mi hija." Roque didn't know then that if he and Maria Antonia had said the word Federalistas, meaning government troops, they would have been shot dead.

Out of nowhere, a feminine voice arose. "Nacho, olvídate del viejo y la chamaca. Nosotros lo que tenemos es hambre. We are just hungry," said the woman in her long flowing skirt and leather boots. Told them to forget the old man and the girl.

Maria Antonia's eyes widened as she saw a rifle lying across her arm. This was no ordinary woman; this one sported a sombrero atop her long-braided hair. And bullet-filled vest crisscrossed her chest and torso.

Nacho looked at her sardonically, then his expression became a sly grin. No doubt he admired her audacity. Then Nacho yelled,

> We may be the poorest of the poor in Mexico, but we are honorable men fighting for an honorable cause. We're not here to molestar a little mocosa and an old man. I see he has plenty of livestock, and we need food for strength to continue our journey.

That day the poorly clad soldiers slaughtered two cows of the handful Roque Menchaca owned. The men devoured the food prepared by female soldiers. The small herd of goats, which had provided life-saving milk for Maria Antonia since birth, also nourished their insatiable appetites.

While chomping on a piece of meat, Nacho exclaimed, "¡Por ser un Gachupín ranchero, tiene mucho y vive bien!"

The disparaging term for Spanish landowners sent a chill up Roque Menchaca's back. Luckily, the same voice that had saved them quickly diverted the attention of the revolutionary. These untrained and uneducated men who had joined Villa's division could hardly be called soldiers. Yet, they had left their daily lives and menial jobs to fight for equality and social justice.

Beset by a series of presidential assassinations, there would be no equality and justice by the time Mexico's Revolution began winding down in 1920. Maria Antonia recalled,

> Although I was just a child, I'll never forget that it was a brave woman who had saved my father and I from harm. This took courage at a time when bands of soldiers as well as revolutionaries marched through villages killed innocent people, and raped young women and girls.

As the future battles and skirmishes raged on for the next several years, villagers and civilians caught in the crosshairs of the revolution would have to be mindful of whether they sprang forth with, "Viva Villa or Vivan los Federales." During the time they took over the ranch, the other women in the group called Maria Antonia's heroine Belén. For the rest of her life, Maria Antonia revered her name. She had rescued her and her father from the frightful encounter with a band of tattered, undisciplined would-be Villa soldiers.

FROM THE START of Mexico's Revolution, women had taken up arms and followed their men into battle. They would come to be called "las soldaderas," or women-soldiers. Mujeres who played a pivotal role in the revolution, serving as soldiers, cooks, and medics.

Some of the women were courageous wives who even brought their children along. Others were girlfriends or concubines. All were heroines because they filled a need whether on the battlefield or at the makeshift camps.

Abuelita asked her grandchildren if they had ever heard of the Adelitas? "¿Has oído de las Adelitas?" On one occasion, when they replied they'd never heard of them, abuela would burst out into a few bars of the revolutionary corrido she had never forgotten.

Si Adelita se fuera con otro,
If Adelita would leave me for another,
La seguiría por tierra y por mar.
I would follow her by land and by sea.
Si por mar en un buque de guerra,
If by sea in a military warship,
Si por tierra en un tren militar.
If by land on a military train.

Maria Antonia stopped to ask if they understood the ways in which historical accounts of the revolution celebrate female soldiers, with songs such as "La Adelita," which came to symbolize their heroic efforts for social justice. In Maria Antonia's eyes, they had proven their worth long before history would assess their contributions and their female Mexican legacies.

Juana Vega brought news and gossip when she went into Muzquiz for food supplies. That fateful day she was not around to experience what Maria Antonia and her father had lived through. Yet she had her own tale to tell.

Juana Vega's return with the news of a peasant uprising confirmed his worst fears.

"Don Roque! ¡La gente pobre se cansó de las injusticias y se han levantado en armas!—The poor got tired and ... took up arms!—¡Dicen que el líder se llama Pancho Villa!—They say their leader is Pancho Villa," Juana Vega said breathlessly. The emergence of Pancho Villa in Chihuahua, and his rapid ascent across Northern Mexico—in the state of Coahuila—had taken Roque Menchaca by surprise.

In May 1911, Villa's first victory in a bloody battle against federal troops in Saltillo was the harbinger of countless battles to come. As leader of the Northern Division of the revolutionary forces, Villa won his most crucial battle in another formidable northern town, Torreon. Meanwhile, earlier in the month of May, Porfirio Diaz had finally abdicated his self-proclaimed throne from which he had ruled Mexico for over thirty years. Upon the dictator's departure, with the support of Francisco "Pancho" Villa and Emiliano Zapata, Francisco I. Madero emerged as Mexico's best presidential candidate.

Having cultivated the friendship of politicians in France, despite the Cinco de Mayo battle that freed Mexico from French intervention, the dictator chose Paris, France, as the city in which to spend his last days in exile. Later, Maria Antonia said she had heard he was buried in Paris.

During the revolution, lack of national, modern communication was one of several factors that inadvertently impacted civilians. So that, according to Maria Antonia, Mexican citizens lived in persistent fear of being killed for being on one side or the other. Civilians had to holler "Villistas" or "Federalistas," depending on which group galloped into town. It was the only way to avert certain death.

Economic depression and political unrest had forced many Spaniards to emigrate to Mexico and elsewhere in the 1800s. Roque Menchaca's parents had left Spain in search of new opportunities and stability in Mexico. The couple was among dozens of Spanish immigrants who chose to start new lives. Ironically, Mexico was increasingly mirroring the country his parents had left. Roque Menchaca noted the cruel irony of immigration. Faced with politicians jockeying for power in Mexico City, and an all-out Mexican Revolution looming, he began to agonize about his only daughter's safety and future.

After pondering the decision his parents had made to emigrate, he even considered escaping with his daughter to Spain, a country he'd never known. After much soul searching, Roque decided the best option was to take Maria Antonia to his sisters. Life in Muzquiz would be safer than on an isolated ranch on Mexico's chaotic northern frontier.

Maria Antonia reluctantly went to the home of Teofela and Enriqueta, her prim and very proper aunts. She would often describe the elegance that awaited her. She said that while her aunts were sympathetic at the loss of her mother, they were dismayed at her primitive behavior. To them, she was like a wildcat. While they understood their brother's concern, they told him Maria Antonia would require a complete restructuring. But they had faith in their plan to educate her so that she could blossom into a distinguished lady under their tutelage. Teofela, the oldest of the two, told Roque Menchaca,

> It's not the poor child's fault that she is so mal educada, uneducated, and uncouth. But we will do everything in our power to help her grow into a proper little lady. Many years later, when I looked back at the teachings of my aunts, I realized I was privileged to have had them take an interest in my breeding. My father was a simple agricultor. He had no wife, and I had no mother to guide me.

Maria Antonia said goodbye to her father amid a river of tears and pleas for him not to leave her. But her anguish quickly turned to wonder and adventure in the lavish home. Teofela and Enriqueta Menchaca observed the acceptable norms of the day, including fashion and etiquette.

Abuela recalled telling her progeny with the strongest demonstration of appreciation for the man who sacrificed his parental role for his daughter's safety.

> I loved my father and I never wanted to leave him. My aunt's assessment of my lack of education must have been true. The first time I saw the large grandfather clock at the top of the stairs, I ran out the door like a cat smarting from being doused with water.

Maria Antonia would reflect on how she came to be brought up by her aunts. She often recalled the long, ruffled dresses her aunts wore. She enjoyed relating her curiosity regarding strange, repressive contraptions they wore underneath their dresses.

Maria Antonia added, "Their ruffled derrieres made a swoosh-ing sound when they walked around. I would always giggle at them and they glared at me with great disapproval."

She spoke about those swooshing days where her aunts dressed in "their S-shaped figures gliding across the room, which always made her wonder about their stiff, molded figures, too." Then, a few weeks before Maria Antonia's fifteenth birthday, "Teofela took an old white dress out of storage." She recalled, "I tried it on, but it didn't fit." So, she altered it for me. Teofela, was more fastidious than her sister. She explained that a dress had to be propped up with contraptions to fit properly and to control a woman's movements. Teofela said all this fashion tediousness had to do with command-ing respect.

The old established Mexican tradition of presenting a young woman to local society at fifteen was called a quinceañera. The un-spoken reason was also to prove the young girl was still a virgin. Since Maria Antonia was going on fifteen years old, her aunts set a date to celebrate with an official party and a special formal dress.

"When I tried it on, it fit perfectly. The S-bend corset she crammed me into pulled everything into place. At last, I had learned the secret behind their S-shaped bodies," she said, throwing her head back in laughter as if she were still that carefree child riding her horse. Maria Antonia's aunts received many compliments on the quinceañera's great success. Locals admired how the two had reared and groomed the child for the past six years. Roque Menchaca, who visited Maria Antonia regularly, was also pleased to see how she had seemingly blossomed into a lady.

Meanwhile, Maria Antonia had no intention of allowing corsets and rigid undergarments to restrain her physically for long. She noted that while her aunts didn't view fashion dictates as self-repression, she did. Nonetheless, she would abide by the dress code out of respect for her aunts. Maria Antonia thought fashion could enslave willing victims. Consequently, at seventeen, she began to reject hoops and dresses in Enriqueta and Teofela's armoires. She thought petticoats were a nuisance. Social demands made her yearn to leave Muzquiz, especially after the death of Esteban Ruiz, her true love.

Although he was no more than a hard-working ranch hand, Esteban Ruiz dreamed of leaving for the United States. Her desire to emigrate may have come from him. Their courtship was not formal. In fact, had her aunts discovered it before his death, they would have objected. Maria Antonia recalled that "Esteban talked about the riches of all estadounidenses. He said it was a nation of immigrants. His uncle had lived in California for many years. And he could attest to the opportunities available for anyone willing to work hard," Maria Antonia said one day, letting her guard down for one moment to talk about her first love. However, she would quickly correct her steps, saying,

> In my youth, we had shame, and we were docile. Yet men respected women. Instead of using our bodies, as many women do today, we used hand-held fans to flirt and attract a young man. We took our fans everywhere we went; we took them to parks, plazas, church and social gatherings.

Her aunts knew Esteban Ruiz's family, so they invited him and other local teenagers to her quinceañera party. Her granddaughters didn't grasp the importance of a hand-held fan, but she said it had helped her communicate with him. Maria Antonia didn't dwell on his memory except to say that were it not for his untimely death she would have married him.

Even if she had felt the deepest love a woman can feel for a man, Maria Antonia would not have revealed this to anyone. Instead, she preferred to relate how compatible they had been before Manuel abandoned her. She said, despite a significant age difference, they got along very well. She would tell her grandchildren,

> As the main accountant for the silver mining company in Muzquiz, Manuel oversaw the payroll. He paid the miners each week. People looked up to him because of his position in the American mining company. My aunts said the poor widower with two children needed a young unmarried woman like me.

Maria Antonia said the courtship began when Manuel started visiting her aunts. He never went to any church socials, but he always found excuses to pay them a visit. It was his way to get to know my aunts before he mentioned his intentions.

She would say, with a hearty laugh, "He was a smart man. Muy listo el hombre and his scheme worked."

Maria Antonia always painted a clear picture of what was expected of young women of her era. Teofela and Enriqueta Menchaca had prepared her for marriage. Her aunts had also stressed that an older man with a promising future or position within a company was the best catch.

Moreover, they argued that a mature man would ensure that a woman and her future children would never go hungry. Maria Antonia's aunts stressed this was especially important in Mexico, a country in which few of its citizens afforded necessities. Interestingly, her father was the only one who questioned the wisdom of this union. "My father's concern was the age difference between Manuel and me. He also felt I was too young to assume responsibility of raising two children who were not my own."

Before her wedding, her father would ask her to think it over. "Toñita, do not marry for any other reason but love. If you love this man, you have my blessing."

"Even though I wasn't sure, I insisted I loved Manuel. With that, my father returned two months later to officially give me away. He was the only one who cried at my wedding."

Maria Antonia loved talking to her granddaughters, especially those who listened.

She'd talk about her wedding day at the youthful age of seventeen. About her wedding dress. She spoke about her padrinos godparents, and bridesmaids who were upstanding citizens of Muzquiz. Her benevolent brown eyes filled with excitement, when she remembered her handmade, white wedding gown. Her aunts had made it from the best material they could find. This made Maria Antonia proud to walk down the aisle, and her father felt gratified to give her away. Father and daughter acknowledged the white wedding gown as evidence of the bride's virginity.

In Michigan, after that horrid Texas experience, reality in the nursing home was riveting. One minute she was recounting her beautiful story and the next she was being prodded by a nurse.

"It's time to take your medicine, Maria."

Confined to a wheelchair, Maria Antonia expressed that she didn't need medicine.

"Yo no necesito medicina. ¿Para qué? What for?"

Then, she would launch into one of her many stories about how she had survived rashes, infections, pneumonia, and even the 1918 Spanish flu simply, by consuming a host of ancient herbal teas, hierbas that her Mexican ancestors took. Among them, cinnamon, hibiscus, and lemon were her favorites.

Memories of growing up in Muzquiz, before it earned official status as a town, were as vivid as if she had just spent a weekend there. Maria Antonia communicated thought-provoking stories about her family members, some of their friends, and occasionally perfect strangers.

One time Maria Antonia shared that one of her many cousins with the propensity for mischief, teased them and their friends about insignificant things until they broke down. Then, she would laugh hysterically at her own exploits. One day, however, this cousin's personality was permanently altered. The family never knew what had happened to her. But in a tiny town like Muzquiz rumors spread that someone had spiked her food or drinks. According to a curandera the family consulted, "this was done with the intent of teaching your relative a cruel lesson." Still, the family couldn't figure out what was wrong. Then, soon enough, the cousin became a fragile and dazed teenager who spent the days swaying in a rocking chair. Maria Antonia expressed that perhaps things like that didn't occur in the United States, but she was cautious just the same. She never consulted curanderas, and didn't trust licensed U.S. medical doctors.

Raising her voice a couple of decibels higher, Maria Atonia recalled, "Mi prima era muy bonita, pero le gustaba reírse de la gente con sus travesuras. My cousin was pretty, but she relied on her mischief to make fun of people." All the while, shaking her head in disapproval, Maria Antonia gave in to the idea that her cousin had been the victim of a mysterious and vengeful prank.

With this tale, Maria Antonia cautioned her grandchildren on the dangers of accepting a doctor's diagnosis as gospel. She honored the Catholic faith, believing in natural healing, and she staunchly held on to the beliefs of her Catholic upbringing. That was one of the reasons she had only seen a doctor once in her lifetime. That was when Anita begged her to see the doctor. She relented—he found nothing wrong with her, and, at the age of one-hundred years, the doctor marveled at her good health. Except for occasional bouts with painful arthritis in her hands, the doctor expressed that there was nothing to worry about.

Another story that intrigued Anita, was abuela's insistence that she had taken care of her father, Jesús Sosa, when he was an infant. Maria Antonia recalled taking care of a baby boy who was temporarily left with her aunts while the widowed father attempted to find a permanent home for the child. The child was the son of a German who had married a young woman from Nueva Rosita who died of tuberculosis. The German, "él alemán," as he was called by locals, began looking for someone to help raise the child while he worked at the local mine. Maria Antonia recalled the baby's name was Jesús, but did not remember the surname because most German surnames were hard to pronounce. The only thing for certain was that his adopted name was Sosa.

Maria Antonia recalled that along with native ethnics, who re-settled from the United States, there was a strong German presence in some Mexican towns. So, it was easy for a child from German heritage to stand out among Mexicans.

She continued,

This German Mexican child, with blond hair and green eyes, was a year old when I first saw him. He had a strange brownish birthmark on his chin and I saw him again at age four. A couple had taken him in, and he still had the birthmark; I remember him because of it. Also, he was taller than most Mexican boys his age.

It would not be until her pregnant daughter returned from Mexico, when Jesús Sosa knocked at the door, that Maria Antonia suspected he had been the one for whom she had cared. His birthmark gave him away.

When Maria Antonia asked him about his background, Jesús told her, "I was adopted and received my stepfather's surname." The possibility that his biological father might have been German never came up. It was his towering six-foot-four-inch frame, his green eyes, and auburn hair that clued in Mexicans that he was German.

Growing up, Anita would try to envision what her father looked like. Because her mother didn't have a single picture of her father, she had no clue as to his appearance. She was told he was fair like Maria Antonia but Anglos in the United States didn't believe he was a Mexican.

Because being fair complected had much currency, by the age of eight, Anita noticed that the peach fuzz on her arms and legs was blond. It was the part of her appearance that compelled her to ask Maria Antonia about her father. One fine day, her grandmother took Anita to a nearby movie theater, featuring movies from Mexico. That was when Anita got an idea about what her father looked like, when Maria Antonia saw and pointed out the tallest, most fair-skinned movie star on the silver screen, and her grandmother whispered.

"¿Ves ese güero? Ese se parece a tú padre." See the tall, fair-haired man up there? He looks like your father. That gave Anita an idea, however vague, about his appearance

Unaware of Mexico's history, and growing up in the United States, Anita wondered what a German was doing in Muzquiz in the 1920s. She had no clue that in the late 1800s Germans started arriving in Mexico to help local businessmen start breweries and other enterprises.

As Anita grew up and began to research Mexico's history, she learned that the United States wasn't the only country that had welcomed foreigners. Indeed, in the early 18th and 19th centuries Mexico welcomed a flood of foreign investors from Spain, France, Germany, and other European nations. Unfortunately, under the guise of investing but with the sole intention of reaping monetary rewards, many of those who descended on Mexico were less interested in remaining and more interested in extracting its riches. Porfirio Diaz is credited with modernizing Mexico and courting foreign investment. For many Mexicans, modernization had been the detriment of its people. And the middle class benefited at the expense of peones, a word used to refer to landless peasants.

Mexico was divided into social classes. Depending on a Mexican's social status, Porfirio Diaz was either a national hero who had improved many areas of Mexico or a heartless, ruthless dictator who had forgotten he had been one of them. Born in the state of Oaxaca, Díaz wanted a capitalist society at any cost. It was in those early years when Diaz set out to modernize Mexico, by building dams, factories, and trains. His iron fist determination relied on repression of the press and its people, earning the slogan, "pan o palo," bread or stick.

Landless Mexicans were too starved and hungry to grasp the benefits of modernization, when all they experienced was heartless foreign corporations stripping natural minerals from their land. To add insult to injury, foreign mine owners, local landowners, and politicians ignored their grievances. Maria Antonia never forgot the bare necessities in her small town before and after the revolution. Once she began living in Muzquiz, her aunts explained why the people had taken up arms. Abuela recalled hearing, "Diaz allowed abuses by foreigners, and he never defended the Mexican people against injustices. Mexicans thought Madero would bring democracy, but he was assassinated."

She explained, "Los Bolillos se aprovechaban de los Mejicanos en su propio país. The Anglos took advantage of Mexicans in their own country. Los discriminaban y muchas veces no les pagaban," they were discriminated, and their pay was withheld without reason. On the other hand, known as criollos, Mexico's privileged class enjoyed their hacienda style of living, unencumbered by the Díaz government. Since Díaz was elected president in 1877, his power remained unabated until 1911.

Indians and working-class mestizos were targeted and a source of hatred for Mexican criollos, who not only enjoyed political and economic power, but also were viewed more favorably because of their appearance—their light complexion associated them with Spanish blood. In the views of the locals, Maria Antonia remembered,

> Los Criollos were no better than the Bolillos. They took advantage of the peones. They exploited and oppressed poor mestizos. In Mexico, you didn't have to be an Indian to feel the humiliation of discrimination—la humillación de ser diferentes.

Muzquiz, Laredo, Monclova, Nueva Rosita, and Piedras Negras were not usual travel destinations for most Americans. For Mexicans entering the United States, these towns were gateways or starting points to reach the proverbial "American dream"—the acquisition of land and home ownership.

Anita was often told by her grandmother that her father was a native of Nueva Rosita, a small town in Coahuila. At the age of twelve, this knowledge inspired her to search for her biological father, despite the odds of ever locating him. From her abuela, she had learned that the state of Coahuila figured prominently in Texas history—under Mexico, the area was known as Tejas Coahuila. Prior to the battle at the Spanish mission of San Antonio de Valero or what is known as The Alamo in San Antonio, Texas, ranches and pueblos kept commercial connection to municipalities such as Saltillo, Monclova, and Muzquiz among others.

Maria Antonia began with the precept that her birthplace was filled with the riches of copper, iron, and other natural minerals. Men from Coahuila worked deep in the bowels of its rich, rocky mines. By contrast, the Menchaca family were part of a privileged, land-owning class who had earned a living as local businessmen.

MARIA ANTONIA was blessed to have reached one-hundred-and-four years free of any sorts of medicine for cholesterol, diabetes, or high blood pressure. As far away as Detroit, medical and nursing home staff were perplexed just as their queries baffled her.

"Whom or what does she credit with keeping her healthy? What's her secret?"

Personnel would often ask anyone who was there to see her, expecting a miracle response. Most recently, another married granddaughter, Rosa Castañeda Bravo, was happy to oblige, for she was just as curious to know. In the ten years she had worked at a Detroit hospital, Rosa had never met anyone as old as her grandmother. However, what astounded her most was not her age, but her incredible lucidity.

When Rosa told her in Spanglish about the inquiries, Maria Antonia retorted.

"You mean to tell me doctors want to know about me? What kinds of questions are they asking? Why don't they come talk to me?"

Her grandmother's reaction made Rosa recognize that any questions about her life were intrusive. Nevertheless, Maria Antonia finally relented. She began by setting the ground rules for a possible interview, cautioning that it must be conducted in Spanish. When Rosa agreed, Maria Antonia looked up at her with a faint smile. Since her granddaughter had not spoken Spanish since childhood, she knew the interviews might not happen after all.

What was most disconcerting for Rosa was her grandmother's way with words. She had a gift for turning even the most educated people into stuttering idiots. When interacting with educated folks, Maria Antonia would reach deep into the crevices of her mind and experiences and relate a fable that left her listeners speechless. This is what was bound to happen to anyone who dared interview her. Rosa, a former Roman Catholic, was now a faith healer who was guided through a Bible-focused religion that stressed scriptures, and her faith had inspired her to seek answers for those who were truly amazed by Maria Antonia's age. At least, toward that end, Rosa succeeded in extracting from Maria Antonia what she thought helped her live to one hundred years of age. After much coaxing, she finally told Rosa,

Before Mexico's Revolution, we lived a very simple, rural life. We planted crops and we ate from our gardens. Our lives were plain and simple and full of hard work. My father had goats that provided milk for me from the time I was born—the milk and the food may be the reason I've lived so long.

Rosa was ecstatic that her grandmother was willing to talk. Unfortunately, Rosa had picked the wrong day as Hilda, her sister, had planned a spectacular birthday party for Maria Antonia, where a letter from President George W. Bush and First Lady Laura Bush would be introduced. Hilda told those preparing for the party, "Abuelita will be taken to the ballroom since many of her children, grandchildren, and great-grandchildren and the rest of the family will be there."

Rosa got up and left, assuring Maria Antonia in "Spanglish" that she would return some other day. Abuela nodded to show she understood, even though she hated being questioned. Rather, she preferred to talk about what she liked to remember most.

At the Michigan nursing home, the word quickly got around that Maria Antonia had questioned the authenticity of the letter from the White House. Ann Perry, head of the nursing staff delighted in teasing abuelita about it and told her.

"We heard you didn't believe President Bush sent you a letter. Well, I don't blame you for doubting it. Nowadays, it could be a hoax."

Perry knew that Maria Antonia didn't speak English. Still, each time she saw her, Perry spoke English to her. Nonetheless, anyone who thought Maria Antonia didn't understand soon found out differently. When addressing someone in English, she might've struggled, but she managed to get her point across.

Kind Care Nursing Home founded in 1951, in Frankenmuth, did not have centenarians until Maria Antonia arrived. She was such a novelty, the entire staff participated in organizing her birthday party. Not all were aware that personal possessions and money were of little use to Maria Antonia, although many of those present brought her a variety of gifts, including money.

Great-grandchildren and grandchildren, who could not speak Spanish, brought Maria Antonia flowers and all sorts of gifts. Some gave her envelopes filled with money, which Maria Antonia received with great joy. Sadly, abuela had not been informed that she was not allowed to have a savings account.

As the emcee, Hilda stood in front of a microphone and hushed the crowd of well-wishers, which included Maria Antonia's first cousin, Melecio Menchaca. He too was in a wheelchair now. His wife said he suffered from Alzheimer's but his face lit up when he saw his long-lost cousin being celebrated.

Maria Antonia exclaimed, "Primo."

Anita delighted seeing abuela's smile widely beaming with joy. She realized primo meant more than just cousin to her abuelita. It was as if she'd just seen a great love that had been lost and was now found. It had been nearly thirty years since they had seen each other.

Soon, Hilda read the brief letter from President Bush to all the attendees, while Maria Antonia looked across to glance at her long-lost cousin. Growing up, they could not have been closer. Melecio, the son of one of Roque Menchaca's brothers, also was raised in Muzquiz.

Melecio was nineteen when he was sent to the United States to live with an uncle after Mexico's revolution. Maria Antonia had not seen him until destiny reunited them in Michigan. Memories of happy times when they played together surfaced for her. She recalled he played the piano like Liberace, however since converting to the Pentecost religion as an adult, he now only played church music when he visited.

In charge of the music, her son, Beto, hired a band that played Mariachi and traditional songs from Maria Antonia's era. After guests finished feasting at the buffet, a giant birthday cake was wheeled into the room, and it was placed on top of a long table in front of Maria Antonia's wheelchair.

The matriarch of this large Mexican American family, Maria Antonia, rose gingerly to speak. As she had done years before at Thanksgiving dinners, abuela reflected on her life. At the holiday meal that brought the family together, no one would have imagined that she'd live to be a centenarian. In her most eloquent Spanish, Maria Antonia began, "I thank all of you for coming to honor a poor, elderly woman like me. I was poor all my life, but rich in the things that really mattered, which were my children and their families." All the while, she had struggled to stand and speak but held tightly to the table on which a three-tiered cake rested.

She tearfully looked at him and said,

> I have had few material possessions, but I had an abundance of love for my children and their progeny. This is what fills my heart with joy now that the end for me is near. It warms my heart to see all of you. I am especially grateful that I still have sight to once again see my dearest cousin, Melecio.

Since Maria Antonia's transfer from Texas to Michigan, nobody in the family had the heart to update her on the new realities. One, her oldest son, Paco, had been killed in an accident in Illinois. Two, her cousin Melecio suffered from Alzheimer's disease.

Overwhelmed by the surprise party, Maria Antonia didn't ask anyone about her oldest son. She may have thought that living in Illinois kept him from attending. She also didn't take note that her cousin's memory had failed in her presence.

Over the years, Paco had been a loving son from the time he was a child until his teenage years. When she crossed the border from Mexico into the United States in 1924, Maria Antonia couldn't have imagined her son would alienate her years later. At one time in this nation's history, immigrants from Mexico had paid a tax to cross over. But Maria Antonia never spoke about a tax. Instead, she recreated the setting and the reason why she and her husband had emigrated. Minerva was a baby and Paco was four when they crossed.

Paco had always been a rebellious son, thumbing his nose at authority and disregarding the rights of others. As a child, his mischief often caused his sister, Minerva, to scream: "Toña, mira a Paco! He's being bad again." But he wasn't bad. He was a prankster. He loved playing the devil's advocate, which didn't sit well with his brothers, his sister, and fellow students in grade school. A decorated war hero, Paco had been wounded as a paratrooper in World War II. With two sons fighting America's wars, Maria Antonia had endured the agony borne by a mother whose sons are at war. While they were overseas, Maria Antonia prayed and attended Mass daily, asking God and a host of saints to spare her two sons.

Because of her limited writing skills, Maria Antonia relied on friends and neighbors to write them letters. But the letters that survived were only those she received from Jeorge.

Unmarried at the time, Jeorge would later tell his mother that those letters kept him going through the hideous fire fights and those battles he endured in World War II and Korea. Anita found the letters inside an old black patent leather purse Maria Antonia never used. She saw the military's return address and the name Jeorge Castañeda, and to ensure they remained grouped together, the letters had been tied with a bright yellow ribbon. Anita honored the content so much it was hard for her to resist the temptation to open even one and read it. When Anita found those letters, she realized how much Maria Antonia had cherished them. Anyone interested in history would have been captivated by the opened parachute encrypted on the upper lefthand corner return address of the worn-out yellow envelopes. Sadly, she found the packet of worn letters after Maria Antonia had been cruelly strapped onto a gurney and taken by force to a San Antonio hospital.

Anita had taken a monthly drive for five years, from Dallas to San Antonio. When she arrived, her grandmother would often be asleep. She had to throw stones at her bedroom window from the driveway to wake her up, hoping and praying she was still alive. For nearly thirty years, Maria Antonia had single-handedly maintained the house. She had fretted about the property taxes, the plumbing, the creaking floors, leaky roof and a host of other desperately needed house repairs. However, regardless of its condition, Maria Antonia was proud to be a homeowner. She delighted in telling anyone who would listen that this was her own home, and that she owed the U.S. government nothing. Her pride sounded like an angry tirade, but she was determined to leave no doubt as to her physical, spiritual, and financial independence.

Abuela often proudly said, "Esta es mi casa, la compre con mi sudor. No necesito nada ni nadie que me de nada. ¿Qué le pido al gobierno? This is my home, bought with my own sweat. I don't need anything from anyone. I don't ask the government for anything!" This preamble usually came in response to her family's request that she apply for social services.

During the five years Maria Antonia lived alone on the top floor of her decayed two-story house, she prayed that Minerva return. Maria Antonia could no longer walk upright. She rejected offers of a walker or wheelchair. Instead, she got around pushing a kitchen chair from one room to another. When her inquilinos owed her rent and failed to pay, Maria Antonia carefully made her way down the stairs to collect it.

On frequent visits to check on her, Anita became her legs and arms. Maria Antonia sent her to pay her utilities and buy food. Because abuela rented out the entire first floor, which had been divided into two apartments, she had to pay cash for all her necessities. However, she was never completely alone. People down and out on their luck, mainly the undocumented, continually sought refuge in her old, dilapidated house.

Income-wise, she depended on a meager social security check of $425, and nominal rent payments to survive. But she never complained about either one. The rental income she received amounted to $45 a week, which she charged a couple who lived together in a two-bedroom unit on the south side of the great old house. Another couple with two children who lived on the first floor on the north end of her spacious house were also charged the same price. Maria Antonia would often say, "The inquilinos respect me."

Over time, Anita persuaded Maria Antonia to accept a charitable service called Meals on Wheels. But abuela was way too proud for her own good. Maria Antonia resisted the service for two years, finally relenting under the weight of her granddaughter's pleas, but this was not without protest. Maria Antonia stubbornly insisted.

> I'm not a charity case. Other people need it more than I do. I have always made my own way in life. Just because I'm old does not mean I can't think and cook for myself.

When you're not here, los inquilinos bring me food or buy
it for me when I give them the money.

In the end, she relented to receive their services. She agreed to
try Meals on Wheels for a few weeks.

One day when Anita arrived to help her with the usual litany
of bills, Maria Antonia announced she would not take any more
food from Meals on Wheels. She took pride in knowing that even
before Minerva had returned to Michigan, she cooked for herself,
as she could never count on her daughter. So, despite arthritic hands
and knees, abuela hoisted herself in front of a white apartment size,
four-burner stove, to prepare her own meals.

In Minerva's absence, Anita made monthly visits to check on
her grandmother. In the humble kitchen, reminders of her eccentric mother were everywhere—from mismatched curtains to an
upside-down picture of Jesus Christ that hung on the wall. She
was embroiled in memories of the chaos. Anita recalled countless
arguments between pragmatic abuelita and eccentric mother.

Maria Antonia and her biological daughter were opposites.
They had little in common. They fought over every little thing.
Minerva, while she seemed not to be all there, as far as the family knew, wasn't mentally ill—she just didn't think about mundane
things the way others did. Still, poor decisions about her life and
the lives of her six children had given her the reputation of being
flighty, bohemian, and lacking common sense. Certain that she was
right and had done no wrong, Minerva never apologized for anything to anyone. As a teenager, she rejected her mother's attempt
to teach her how to prepare tasty dishes—she hated to cook. Maria
Antonia wondered how she fed her six children. Throughout her life
she had given her daughter moral and financial support. In the end,
Minerva moved to Texas, as living with Maria Antonia guaranteed
her the freedom from family responsibilities.

When she bought her Michigan home, Maria Antonia had
hoped to live there the rest of her life. But her son and his wife
had bought ten acres and begun building a new home without her
knowledge, and she reluctantly agreed to move in with them. Abuela

had not been privy to the purchase they had made upon the high school graduation of their oldest daughter. The move meant selling the house Maria Antonia had bought while he was at war. Jeorge, his wife and their growing brood, appeared happy to have abuela stay on. Still, the revelation of the sale left her feeling betrayed, even when she received her share of the sale from the house.

With money she had saved and the sale, Maria Antonia amassed enough money to buy a place, albeit a condemned house. To make sure she had enough money, before leaving Michigan abuela cashed in her life insurance policy.

There was never a time in her life that Maria Antonia was ever broke. She always had money.

From the moment the two women entered the abandoned house, Maria Antonia began thinking of ways to restore the property to its turn-of-the century grandeur. She encouraged her daughter to look beyond the precariously tilted house in ruins. Minerva argued with Maria Antonia about the renters throughout the three decades Maria Antonia rented out the ground floor of her dilapidated house south of downtown San Antonio. Minerva complained the tenants always paid the rent late. That these poor sleazy folks took advantage of Maria Antonia despite the cheap rent. Minerva often shouted her concerns to her mother in Spanish, to ensure everyone heard and understood.

> You rent the house to just anybody. You don't know who
> they are. Many times, they don't pay the rent on time, and
> you let them remain here anyways. You can't feel sorry for
> them just because they're here illegally. This is a business
> like any other. People must pay when payment is due.

Maria Antonia's compassion for her inquilinos did not allow her to listen. "Pobrecitos," she would murmur in defense of those who took refuge in her old home. Minerva's point of view often collided with her mother's. One example that led to frequent discord was Maria Antonia's insistence on renting the tiny house deep in the depth of a huge backyard.

Despite their differences, Maria Antonia struggled to understand Minerva. She never could see why Minerva left her first husband. The U.S. Army veteran that had fathered Mercedes before he was deployed to Europe during World War II. When he returned, the two stayed together long enough to impregnate her with Martha and celebrate her second birthday. By the time the mother and daughter agreed to leave Michigan, Maria Antonia had learned to accept her excuses for a failed marriage, as well as her illicit births. She felt compassion for the challenges her daughter faced as a widow. Truth be told, in her heart of hearts, Maria Antonia knew that Minerva was responsible for much of the chaos in her life.

LIKE BOTH HER PARENTS, Minerva was born in Muzquiz, Coahuila in 1924. Her migration story began as an infant. Maria Antonia crossed the border with Minerva in her arms when she was nine months old. She recalled being a quiet and obedient little girl who didn't give any trouble. Some people assumed she was mute.

Minerva always said that she took after Manuel Castañeda, her father—an intellectual who loved to read. She adored her father and felt a great loss when he left them. However, she never held him accountable and blamed Maria Antonia's personality for his abandonment. Still, she had more positive memories of him. Manuel was an affectionate father who often bragged about Minerva's self-taught ability to read and write Spanish, despite the institutional barriers and language prejudice in Dallas's schools.

Because of the family's migratory pattern, Minerva missed many years of schooling. Yet, she forever remained a lover of books and never gave up reading. Agricultural work was something she resented and resisted, instructing her daughters that they would never be subject to work in the fields, as she promoted education for them. Minerva's dislike for picking whatever was in season was so intense that she would run away from her duties to find a place to rest. There, she sat in the middle of the field until her mother retrieved her. Maria Antonia shamed her with a comparison to her brothers' work production, lauding them for being hard workers, unlike her who was lazy.

Maria Antonia showed predilection for her boys and was tougher on Minerva. Gender differences between daughter and brothers would emerge. Minerva never forgot the time her mother shamed her when she noticed Minerva's breast development. She detested Maria Antonia's sense of humor and found it unacceptable. She perceived it as disgusting. Another shortcoming she disliked about Maria Antonia was that she never discussed feminine hygiene, and menstruation was never a topic of discussion between them. Her first time was frightening and associated it with a memory of running from the classroom in fear and embarrassment.

Minerva married her first husband in the old red-brick courthouse in Dallas. This official union had produced Mercedes and Martha López. Later she married Ricardo Peña, her third husband, who didn't drink. However, because the church refused to annul his marriage in Mexico, they officially married when their third child was born.

The fear of being trapped inside a loveless marriage led Minerva to live with Jesús Sosa while she was in Mexico. She had traveled there to visit her father, Manuel. Instead of finding her father, Minerva hit upon Jesús.

Already pregnant, after the two lived together in Mexico, Minerva returned to the United States. When she left, Jesús found a goodbye note. So, he packed up and headed north. The first time he crossed the border, Jesús was a fourteen-year-old boy, and knew the ways of crossing, having made the journey many times without documents. Jesús told abuela that nobody stopped him because he represented cheap labor. In fact, the last time he crossed the international bridge, he bragged that the guards waved at those who entered to do daily to work in the United States.

A widowed grandmother of four now, Minerva yearned for a new love. Her young face fooled people into thinking she was thirty something. Abuela was a seventy-two-year-old great-grandmother whose hard life made her look older than her age. While not physically beautiful, Minerva felt beautiful. Despite a wide face and a nose reflecting her Indian heritage, she flaunted her femininity. Lack of physical beauty didn't stop her from having romantic dalliances.

She failed to focus on repairing the condemned house Maria Antonia had bought. Instead, Minerva began dating a man twenty-years younger.

Abuela recalled that Minerva arrived in Michigan emaciated and discouraged from having left the man she loved in Mexico. Later, Minerva would claim that her true everlasting love was Jesús who gave her their love child—Anita. Jesús Sosa won in the end, persuading Minerva to take their newborn and begin life anew. During their relationship in Michigan, the couple argued. He was angry that his child didn't carry his surname. A physical confrontation led the couple to separate on Anita's fifth birthday.

From abuelita, Anita learned that Jesús Sosa had been deported under a program called Operation Wetback while at work. After hearing that story countless times, Anita vowed to petition for his legal entry when she became of age. She didn't know that, without a birth certificate proving a father and daughter relationship, her case would not prevail in the courts.

When she separated from Jesús, Minerva wasted no time finding the next man in her life. When she realized that the love of her life would not return, she began dating Ricardo Peña, who had documents that authorized him to work in the United States. This Colima, Mexico, native, with a portly build and amiable personality became her official, legal husband in 1957. By that time the couple had become parents of a third child. Minerva had two daughters from the first husband, one from the man who was deported, and three from a husband who left her widowed. Widowhood appeared to be the answer to her instability and restlessness, for Minerva resolved to stay single from that day forward.

Except for Mercedes, by the early 1950s the rest of her children had been born in Michigan. Not all newly arrived Mexicans were undocumented migrants. In fact, many were born in the U.S. or had passports and permanent residency also known as green cards, which allowed them to work and establish residency. Of those who arrived, some began businesses, others worked for General Motors.

Long before Minerva became a widow, she swore her children would be high achievers. An avid reader and collector of good books, despite only having had an eighth-grade education, Minerva often blamed her mother for depriving her of a formal education. When she chose to travel from state-to-state in pursuit of backbreaking migratory work, Minerva's dream was to be middle class.

Books were the way to achieving her dream. She made up for her lack of education by embracing the printed word, pursuing knowledge in all its forms at a time when Mexican migrants in the United States felt blessed to have work and put food on the table. Her thirst for knowledge of history, social studies, classical music, and the arts led to her transformation. Minerva rejected her social status. She did all she could to transform into a self-educated intellectual. Had it not been for her desire to soar above her socioeconomic status and racial discrimination, her oldest daughters would not have had ballet or piano lessons, which exposed her and the children to the performing arts. Family members were astounded to see her plunge into a lifestyle traditionally reserved only for America's Anglo middle-class families.

Long before the term was bandied about, Minerva was a renaissance woman.

After consuming books on health, medicine, and psychology, she initiated home rules aimed at helping her children prepare to live better lives. While bringing up her six children, with a third husband in tow, she refused to allow television in her home. She felt modern technology interfered with logic. In her view, it hindered free thought. She not only banned television, going as far as to declare it worthless, she also prohibited certain magazines, strongly believing that parents must feed their children's knowledge, and that mental nourishment could not be found in gossip columns, glitzy Hollywood magazines, or television.

Within this tenet, Minerva often argued that "Magazines are full of Hollywood gossip, which is garbage," and vehemently chastised the reading of such material, asking, "Why would you want to read about the lives of these people? Books are available for free! You should seek knowledge that will open doors. Never forget, knowledge is power."

Premised on her organic intellectual beliefs, a home rule she launched early in her children's upbringing was that they visit the local library. So it was that her daughters would often return with armloads of books every Saturday. She often sermonized. "You need to go to the library every week." Her daughters would spend many hours reading books. Some were usually above their grade level at school. Her mantra imparted that knowledge is crucial. It's a weapon against ignorance and will lead to a better life than she had growing up.

In her old German-built home in Saginaw, Michigan, it was not uncommon to find her three oldest daughters sitting on top of metal heat registers reading. Prose and poetry books warmed their minds and hearts, while the heat from a basement furnace warmed their shivering young bodies. She never tired of telling her children, "You don't want to be a migrant! You don't ever want to pick cotton like I did. I hated working like a slave in the cotton fields."

Although Maria Antonia had raised her four children in the Roman Catholic faith, Minerva didn't accept the teachings of the church without question. She joined the Rosicrucian organization based in San José, California, by U. S. mail.

When information arrived from the metaphysical, mystical group sometimes perceived as a cult, she devoured it. She yearned to know all about the spiritual self. She also thought this too would benefit her girls, so she introduced her three oldest daughters to these principles. Later, as Mercedes became a teenager, Minerva began buying not only books about success, but records on positive thinking. The girls never forgot Earl Nightingale's voice reading from Napolean Hill's book, "Think and Grow Rich." He'd say, "You become what you think about," repeating "Let me say that again" and he would.

But all was not about books, when her daughters were not reading something that increased their knowledge of history, geography, and science, the girls were expected to cook and clean the house.

They absorbed Hill's philosophy while doing their chores. Years later, her daughters could recite verbatim what the speaker said in that, "Think and Grow Rich" record.

When Anita, Mercedes, and Martha López told Maria Antonia the things their mother was teaching them, she would howl with laughter. Then, in perfect Spanish and shaking her head in disbelief, Maria Antonia told them, "Your mother must be crazy to think all those things she is discovering are going to do you any good."

In her own way and, perhaps out of love for her granddaughters, or because her own daughter was so convincing, Maria Antonia paid for the ballet lessons. She loved watching the girls perform on stage, especially in ballet recitals where parents and friends saw what they had achieved. She helped in other ways. Abuela's knowledge of sewing and embroidery, which her aunts had taught her, came in handy when it came to sewing costumes for school plays, Christmas pageants, and patriotic social gatherings in which the girls participated.

She basked in the applause, as if it was for her, instead of her granddaughters. Almost a home-schooling teacher, Minerva was relentless, lecturing her girls on the beauty of being a ballerina. She told them this was a career requiring discipline in several steps. For one, they had to practice to the point of exhaustion. Second, they had to focus on posture and grace, even when not in ballet school. She wanted her daughters to simulate those figures exhibited in those Degas' posters of ballerinas hanging on the wall. She forever reminded her daughters:

> When you become a ballerina, you must take care that your body remains in harmony with your weight. You cannot allow yourself to gain pounds your feet cannot withstand. Take care to push away bread, potatoes, candy, and other foods that will diminish your ability to dance, as a prima ballerina must.

Through her three oldest daughters, Minerva was living out her dreams. Martha, her outspoken daughter, compared her mother to

Mama Rose—the mother of Gypsy Rose Lee the famous burlesque queen—who was as dominant as Minerva.

One day, Mercedes and Martha finally rebelled: "We don't want to be ballerinas! We quit ballet classes!"

Minerva was disappointed enough to hear her two oldest daughters did not want to become ballerinas, but when Anita quit, her mother was devastated. Shattered, Minerva listened to what the girls wanted. Mercedes longed to be a missionary; Martha a filmmaker; and Anita an English teacher or writer. Mercedes had been inspired by the Dominican nuns while volunteering at their convent. She did not move into the convent but found excuses to volunteer with daily chores. The religious order had offered Mercedes the peace she could not get at home. Soon she talked about becoming a nun so she could help the less fortunate in poor countries. Mercedes was a straight A student, and a member of the National Honor Society, she received a four-year scholarship to attend Michigan State University.

Anita imagined becoming a writer. Martha was the avid reader. Some of the authors she talked about with Anita quenched their thirst to travel. She talked about Jane Austen, Charles Dickens, and Washington Irving. But she was also fascinated by authors foreign to family members, such as Victor Hugo, Alexandre Dumas, and Honoré Balzac. Although well read, unlike Anita, Martha never shared her desire to be a writer. In fact, she would announce she wanted to be a Hollywood producer one year, and the next to join the Peace Corps. Family members attributed Martha's lack of direction to adolescence, and were convinced she would decide what to do with her life once she reached high school graduation. No one suspected mental illness.

When she turned twelve, Martha rebelled and her stubborn behavior resulted in beatings. She began breaking the rules and brought home magazines she knew were banned. She wore heavy makeup and short skirts, both of which were prohibited at the Catholic school they attended.

The fact that all three of her daughters stopped their ballet lessons didn't sit well with their mother. Enraged, she promptly declared they were not going anywhere for now. Urged by the need to redirect her children, Minerva involved the girls in spiritual experiments, presumably those she learned from the Rosicrucian teachings to which she turned for help. The experiments were harmless. They were an attempt to prove to her daughters the true existence of spiritual energy. She said the Catholic Church called this energy saints. By now she had abandoned the teachings of the Catholic faith. She said the church preferred they not know about spiritual energy. Thus, the church had chosen to assign individual saint names to it.

This is how she explained the ghosts that visited her children in the large German-built home she and her third husband bought. And it was this two-story haunted house, with a foreboding organ in the vestibule, that prompted her to pursue teachings of the Rosicrucian's.

Ricardo Peña, a mild-mannered man from Mexico who had arrived in Michigan in the late 1940s, also came in search of the proverbial American dream. He was a peaceful soul endowed with a beautiful voice, regardless of what he was doing on any given day he would sing. With Ricardo Peña, music became central in their lives. Known for spontaneously launching into a song, the children learned Mexican corridos or ballads and romantic songs popularized by Pedro Infante and Jorge Negrete. Although abuela didn't like the idea of a stepfather for her three granddaughters, Ricardo Peña's fun-loving character won her and the family over. Ricardo was an amazing father. He had no malice in his bones. He adored all his children. From him, Mercedes, Martha, and Ana López learned to make Mexican dishes considered foreign to most non-Mexican residents in the tiny Michigan town.

He loved to cook, making dishes from his native Mexican region from scratch. He had tried teaching Minerva how to make pinto beans cooked in fried Mexican sausage known as chorizo. He also knew how to make soft white flour tortillas. Then, there was no such thing as store-bought ones in Michigan. His attempt to show Minerva how to cook failed at every turn. The two had met at a local dance after she'd given up hope of seeing Jesús Sosa ever again. Ricardo Peña spoke no English, but his excellent Spanish attracted her.

Jeorge, who had returned from the war, and his brother, Beto, worked at GM, alongside their future brother-in-law. The three men worked there during the height of America's love affair with the automobile. Beto had not been drafted or enlisted in military service. At nineteen, he married his high school sweetheart. Eager to assume his responsibilities, he went to work at the GM plant. He and his brother were faithful employees for fifty years. Ricardo Peña was a skilled butcher, a profession he enjoyed, when he was hired as a blue-collar assembly worker by General Motors in Saginaw.

After eight years, Ricardo Peña would not reap GM's rewards. His untimely death provided Minerva hefty death benefits. It was prior to his death, and after Minerva had given birth to her fourth daughter, that the couple bought the haunted house in Saginaw. It was not until the birth of her first son, followed by the birth of another daughter, that she married Peña in a civil ceremony. The two-story house became home to their six children, and Minerva.

Had Ricardo Peña not died, leaving three children ages seven, three, and two, Anita was certain that their lives would have been stable. But insecurity began as soon as their mother was left widowed, and she began planning a permanent move to California. Without consulting anyone, she placed an ad in the local newspaper that resulted in the sale of all the home's furniture, including bedding and decorative items. Narcissic to the core, Minerva didn't ask eighteen-year-old Mercedes, sixteen-year-old Martha or thirteen-year-old Anita about moving across the country. Driven by her impulses, Minerva sold her household belongings, and except for Mercedes López drove to California with them. Unbeknownst to her children, Minerva's goal was to pay a personal visit to Rosicrucian headquarters in San José.

Ricardo Peña's life insurance gave her wings to fly. And, with her children in tow, she vacated their spacious house to explore spiritualism. Mercedes López received a letter spelling out the details of the renewal of her scholarship to Michigan State University. That letter spared Mercedes López from the odyssey.

Minerva had always been a magnet for the opposite sex. She didn't need to flash a smile or flirt to get attention. A well-preserved woman, she was obsessed with retaining her youth. Her five-foot, two-inches frame was as solid as a rock, despite having given birth to half a dozen children.

In fact, having read several books on the benefits of certain herbs and oils, Minerva concocted her own face cream, hand lotion, and life enhancing liquid foods, in hopes of ensuring her health and vitality. Every day, convinced of the benefits, she would grind and pulverize fruits and vegetables. Often, she reminded her girls of the importance of virtually every vitamin on the market and credited her multi-vitamin intake for her impeccable skin and lack of wrinkles, despite her ascent into senior citizen status. She could literally recite each vitamin's purported health benefits, having dedicated herself to that.

Long before news reports warned of the dire effects of sun exposure, Minerva had warned her daughters about the dangers of losing vital natural oils to sun exposure. Consequently, when she and members of her family moved to Texas, her warnings escalated. Without anyone soliciting her opinion, she readily gave advice.

> Always wear long sleeves in the brutal Texas sun. That's what I did as a child, picking cotton in the hot sun. Others laughed at me for doing that, but I knew the sun was harmful to the skin. I read about its effects, and I knew the sun was bad if you were in direct sunlight all day—like we were.

There is no doubt Minerva was self-centered. In the most holistic way, she was consumed with self-adulation. Of course, to the casual observer, her mission was to live her life the way she saw fit. The way she thought was best for her. Perhaps thinking no one else did, she had learned to love herself.

In defense of her life choices and marital status, and in contradiction to what she told her daughters, Minerva compared herself to sexy Hollywood stars to justify her behavior. To defend her lifestyle, although she did not support the reading of Hollywood magazines, she was known to tell her teenaged daughters,

Look at all those Hollywood movie stars. They don't care what anyone thinks. Movie stars live their lives for themselves. So why can't I? Look at Elizabeth Taylor. Look at Zsa Zsa Gabor—they were each married more than three times!

Her daughters were bewildered by her reasoning. As they grew, they too became as disappointed with their mother's disregard for social norms, as abuelita.

Maria Antonia staunchly disapproved of the way in which Minerva ridiculed social rules. She viewed her daughter as an irrational woman. Abuela said Minerva didn't care about shaming the family. Thus, Minerva became a prickly thorn on her mother's side as one who throughout her life fought for and cherished morality and honor.

"What can I do? Minerva is my only daughter. Now that she's a young widow, she's become a libertine who thinks that's what it means to be independent," Maria Antonia would lament years before they traveled together to find a new home in San Antonio, Texas. Abuela continued, "I know she's out of touch with her proper place in life. She left her first husband, Manuel López, as soon as he returned from World War II. After Jesús Sosa crossed Mexico's border, she made excuses and found someone to forget him once he was deported. It was Ricardo Peña's death that finally convinced her marriage was not for her."

Now, as Anita listened to abuela's birthday speech, she too was struck by her astonishing memory. Her body was as fragile as Waterford crystal, requiring help from a staffer to rise to her feet. To recall her exodus from Mexico, she didn't need any help. Looking around at her family, she once again reiterated,

When I left that unstable country, I never looked back. I was convinced we were leaving a country that would always be led by generals and politicos embroiled in war and injustice. I didn't want that country for my children. With Minerva in my arms, and Paco at my side, I came here with my husband and his children. I don't regret coming.

Anita marveled at the beautiful way in which the nursing home staff decorated the ballroom for Maria Antonia's birthday. Her care stood in stark contrast to the San Antonio nursing home in which she was first placed.

On the day Maria Antonia was forced out of her home, Anita didn't arrive in time to stop the court-ordered action by the Texas Department of Social Services. A state counselor had joined forces with a state-funded doctor to conclude that Maria Antonia could no longer live alone, especially in a house slightly tilted in a southerly direction. Abuela never worried about the foundation of her home. She always defended her decision to buy it and marveled at its solid construction. Even family members who visited and noted the dangerous foundation problems never succeeded in convincing Maria Antonia to fix it. She recalled her daughter persuading her in a different direction.

> Minerva took me to see modern homes when we arrived. I saw walls that looked like nothing but cement board. One swift kick and you'd put a hole in it. Most were built of a wood-like panel. Even if I could have afforded one, I didn't want a new, elegant modern home.

In Maria Antonia's view, there was no reason to rebuff old, dilapidated houses. Maria Antonia would say, "If we were able to live in a broken-down shack provided by the farmers for whom we worked as migrants, we could've lived anywhere." Maria Antonia told everybody, "The benefit here is there's running water and an inside bathroom on both levels of this old house. She added, "when Minerva and I found it, the house was all boarded up." She often told renters and family,

> I could see through the cobwebs and boards, and it looked exactly like my first house in Michigan. The walls and floors are solid wood. Unlike modern homes made from nothing but paper, my home is sturdy. I know modern homes won't withstand tornados and other disasters, but mine will.

From her late 20s into her early 60s, to raise her children and remain independent, Maria Antonia worked most any job. As she slowly aged, her knees began buckling under her weight. Family members suggested she see a doctor about her rheumatoid arthritis. Maria Antonia rejected their idea.

Abuela was a fearless woman, who often said that hard work is what defines a man or a woman, emphasizing that money obtained through hard work and the strength of your body was honorable. Work is not something to be ashamed of regardless of what it is. Then she would raise her hands to underscore what she meant.

At the old house in Texas, the time came when she stopped tending to her garden, when the flight of stairs caused her heart to race and left her breathless. Her ensuing frailty led Anita to contact the Texas Department of Social Services to request an occasional visit to Maria Antonia. However, Anita never suspected the state-run agency was powerful enough to decide the fate of a centenarian. More shocking to her was that it would conspire with health officials, and a municipal judge would even issue a court order removing abuela from her own home. Anita agonized,

> This is all my fault! Why didn't I just ignore abuelita's need for special attention? Why did I ever trust a government-run agency to check on her? Hadn't she always rejected involving any organization in her affairs? Now, I'm faced with what they have the power to do to her.

After their intervention, a San Antonio ambulance was dispatched to an unsuspecting Maria Antonia, while Anita tended to the needs of her own family. Nevertheless, she blamed herself for her grandmother's predicament.

Abuela fiercely coveted her independence right into her centenarian existence. She declined to have food delivered, albeit her shaky hands prevented her from holding on to a frying pan, skillet, or even a cup of coffee without spilling its contents. As she was preparing to leave San Antonio to return to her North Texas home, abuela often told Anita, "Hija mia please do not close or tighten the lids on jars or the milk bottle before you leave me. My arthritis won't allow me to open anything painlessly."

Abuela was selfless, preferring to help her family rather than have them help her—she never called her sons to complain. And, at ninety-eight, she was left to fend for herself.

DURING THE FIVE YEARS Minerva lived in Michigan, she often called on Maria Antonia to ask for money. Anita witnessed these requests when she called her to complain she had no money for dental care or doctor visits. She grumbled that her social security check was not enough to live on despite help from Ricardo Peña's three children. To express her concern, in Spanish, Anita pleaded,

> Abuelita, she abandoned you! I know she's my mother, so I know how she is and how she's been! And, after how she's behaved, you should not send her money for anything. I can't believe that, of all people, she asks you for money! She knows how little you get in social security!

Anita reminded Abuela that in a fitful rage her mother had left her. She also took the car Maria Antonia had paid for in cash and left the state with the child she had adopted. Even those who rented Maria Antonia's "casita" in the back of her house could not believe her daughter had moved away. Yet, Minerva shamelessly persisted asking for money. Again, Maria Antonia took pity on her and explained her behavior to her granddaughter.

> Minerva is my only daughter, and she needs help. I have never approved of her life choices, but she's still the child who formed in my womb. I can never abandon her, even though she has not been a good daughter, and even though she abandoned me.

Anita was caught in the middle. Still, based on what she had seen and heard growing up, Anita didn't think her mother deserved financial help. For one, this was not the first time Maria Antonia had rescued her. Each time she got the urge to "andar la seca y la meca," Maria Antonia came to the rescue. Sadly, Anita never heard her mother thank Maria Antonia for helping her raise her daughters. Instead, Minerva spent her life berating abuelita. Maria Antonia had been very strict with her growing up. Still, this was not the justification for treating her mother with a great deal of dislike and resentment.

Even when the two women agreed to live together in the dilapidated and condemned San Antonio home, Minerva never ceased to chastise her mother. Although she never came right out and said she hated her, Anita felt no love lost.

Anita's eyes welled up, recalling the heart-wrenching day Maria Antonia was taken from her own home. It was the first time she had been physically restrained. She felt as if she'd been arrested for a crime she had not committed. As for the Texas authorities, they left a message on Anita's cellphone simply stating that a court order had been obtained to authorize hospitalization for Maria Antonia. They didn't mention abuela had been strapped to a gurney. Neighbors said the two men who took her away looked mean.

The news of abuelita's situation could not have come at a worse time. Anita's Audi was in a local garage being serviced, so she frantically rushed to a local car agency to get a rental car, because she needed to drive from Dallas to San Antonio, to rescue her grandmother before it was too late.

Anita couldn't just leave without an explanation. She had to notify her husband who was out of town on business, arrange to have her youngest son picked up at school, and notify her oldest son away at college. She also had to pack a suitcase for at least an overnight stay. The convenience of living in a north Dallas suburb helped speed up what she regarded then as a lifesaving situation. She knew there was not a minute to waste. Unfortunately, five hours later, when she arrived at her abuelita's home, she was gone.

One longtime renter said in Spanish, while wiping away his tears. "We saw the whole thing. Two men came in an ambulance and strapped her to a gurney. Then they shoved the gurney into an ambulance. Your grandmother didn't cry out. She just laid there motionless and in shock." Just then, Anita's cellphone rang. It was a social worker calling to say Maria Antonia was now at the Santa Rosa Hospital emergency room. The social worker told her she could come see abuelita but could not get her grandmother released as a doctor was evaluating her. She did not say she'd be transferred to a nearby nursing home.

Anita screamed over the phone to the social worker, as she headed to her car.

> Why are you doing this to my grandmother? My grand-
> mother is deaf and doesn't speak English very well, but
> she's not sick. You don't have the right to come into her
> home and take her to the hospital against her will.

The social worker remained calm and told Anita there was nothing she could do. The agency and the doctor had decided it was in Maria Antonia's best interest, since she had been living alone without a guardian or anyone nearby to care for her.

Anita knew where Santa Rosa was located. She had seen the hospital from the highway each time she visited her grandmother. So, after hanging up on the social worker, she cranked up the engine and headed there. She was filled with a horrible fear for her beloved abuelita as she drove through downtown San Antonio to get there.

She stopped crying long enough to realize that the first person she should call was her mother, Minerva. Anita wept while dialing the phone number, as she drove with one hand on the steering wheel, and her cellphone in the other.

> Mom. Mom. I'm calling you to let you know they've taken
> grandma away by force! I rented a car and drove here to the
> hospital where the Texas Department of Social Services
> brought her for evaluation. They used a court order issued
> by a local judge to take her from her home.

Anita continued breathlessly explaining to her mother that while she knew the Texas authorities had been monitoring her to ensure abuela was safe in her home and in good health. She never imagined they'd take her away. Her mother's response left her speechless. Minerva sounded as resentful of her mother as ever.

Good, I'm glad they took her away! She belongs in a nursing home. It's her fault I moved back to Michigan. One of her renters didn't like me. When I threatened to evict her, Toña sided with her. That's when I had had enough.

It was always about her. Anita couldn't believe the depth of her animosity toward Maria Antonia. It had only been a few months since her grandmother had responded to her cry for financial help. By now, she thought her mother would have forgiven Maria Antonia for whatever she had done.

Anita told Minerva, "Listen to me, mom! You sent us older kids to a Catholic school, where they taught us about forgiveness. Don't you see that whatever abuelita did to you does not justify your treatment?" Anita screamed, "She's your MOTHER!"

Minerva yelled back on the phone:

I know what the Bible says. It says forgive them and forget them. I forget about everyone after I have forgiven them. So, don't tell me about forgiveness. Catholics are hypocrites anyway. I'm so sorry I sent you girls to Catholic schools. Those nuns were not very nice. They were prejudiced. They never liked Mexicans.

Anita Lopez shouted, before hanging up,

I'm sorry for you, mom. You have never wanted to see what we all see. You have never taken a good look at yourself. You've never changed. You have always interpreted the Bible to suit yourself. You never cared about how we, your children, felt about things. You always did what was good for you. And only you.

Minerva never said why she and her mother always argued. Bits and pieces blurted out in anger, that led family members to believe Maria Antonia had been a tyrannical disciplinarian. Still, anyone who knew Maria Antonia often spoke of her in warm, glowing terms.

YEARS BEFORE Maria Antonia moved away from the home she had shared with her son, Jeorge and his large family, Anita heard that her mother threaten her grandmother with deportation. She didn't know what ignited the argument, but she never forgot the word deportation. Although she was just a youngster, Anita recalled that during those heated arguments Minerva threatened her grand-mother with los federales. Mercedes and Martha heard her too.

Self-consumed, Minerva never realized she was verbally abus-ing Maria Antonia in their presence. Of course, Minerva didn't say the word "deportation." She didn't need to say it. Saying she'd call "los federales" or the federal government implied she would have Maria Antonia sent back to Mexico and this was clearly understood even by a child.

If Maria Antonia tried to insist on something, if she opposed something, or suggested or questioned Minerva about the mari-tal status of the father of her three youngest children, she would go into a rage once again threatening to call "la inmigración." She would shout at Maria Antonia, telling her she had crossed the bor-der without papers, warning her that she'd have to leave if federal authorities found out. They all recalled the threats. "Tu viniste aquí sin papeles y vas a ver cuándo les llame a los federales. Tú tendrás que irte de este país."

Maria Antonia not only defended herself but was defiant. She usually stated with great pride that two of her sons had fought for this country. For her, that was justification enough for calling the United States her home. She dared her daughter to call the Immi-gration and Naturalization Services. "Llámale a los federales. No les tengo miedo. Mis hijos son veteranos y la ley me ampara," she would reply in Spanish, challenging Minerva to turn her into the immigration authorities. Family members and friends were dismayed to hear Minerva hurl such brutally offensive accusations.

Maria Antonia would triumphantly tell her daughter, "Yo no tengo miedo. I'm not afraid. Llámale a los federales—call the Feds. Yo trabaje. Compre mi casa. Pago mis impuestos … I bought my house and paid my taxes. ¡Así que no tengo miedo!" I'm not afraid.

Those heated arguments between mother and daughter usually took place in the home she shared with Jeorge. But one day, Jeorge walked in precisely when his sister was yelling at the top of her lungs threatening to call the immigration and naturalization services on their aging mother. When he heard his mother defending herself, Jeorge stepped into the fray to defend her. He clenched his fists as he spoke, burning a hole in his sister's face while ordering her out of his house.

> Who do you think you are? How dare you come over here
> and talk to our mother like that! Just because you have
> a green card doesn't make you better. My mother has as
> much right to be here as you do.

The oldest of Minerva's daughters were very close to their grandmother. When they heard about their uncle banning their mother from his house, not only did they worry about seeing their grandmother again, but also wondered what their mother had done to provoke their uncle.

Aside from missing Maria Antonia's kisses and loving embraces, the girls worried about loss of affection, culture, and lifestyle. Were it not for abuela, they would never have baked Christmas cookies each year. They would never have enjoyed Spanish-language movies, the annual circus, the annual fair. Although she didn't understand English, Maria Antonia still took the girls to see The Ten Commandments.

With the passage of time, however, mother and daughter patched up their differences. Like a war in which both sides agree to a temporary ceasefire, before too long, the two were on speaking terms. One secret to family peace was that Maria Antonia was as thick-skinned as an armadillo. She knew if she raised the white flag of peace, both she and Minerva's children would benefit immensely.

Like so many children privy to arguments between adults, Anita grew up perplexed over their disagreeable relationship. Minerva had never demonstrated any physical affection for her mother or her own children, and she often berated Maria Antonia for stripping her of their love. Anita and her sisters grew up under their mother's iron-fisted pronouncements. They could not question or show disrespect to her in any way. Even the most minimal attempt to question or challenge her authority was met with anger, coupled with the menacing index finger. If she was enraged, one, or all three of her daughters, would get a good thrashing with whatever was handy.

Minerva did not hesitate to threaten whichever daughter had the audacity to ask a personal question.

Why are you asking me questions about Toña? She's just your grandmother. I'm your mother and you must do as I say. I know how she really is and who she really is. You had better be quiet or you will see who I am.

Mercedes, Martha, and Anita would talk amongst themselves, questioning and wondering whether all the awful things their mother shouted at Abuela were true.

Was their grandmother undocumented? Had she broken some law? If so, was this a crime?

"Do you think abuelita came here illegally?" Anita would ask her two oldest sisters.

"If she did, she is in big trouble," Mercedes authoritatively assured her, with Martha poised to arrive at her own conclusion.

I don't think she did anything wrong! She came here in 1924 with her husband. Some history books I've read said many Mexicans came to the United States after the Mexican Revolution. And I think abuelita is right about her sons fighting for this country. That should have earned her citizenship!

In the end, the three agreed it didn't matter. Abuelita had showered each of them with so much love and attention nothing their mother said about her could change that. So, they kept silent about the hurtful words their mother had spoken. The respect and love for their grandmother won out.

Even as both mother and daughter aged, Minerva never spoke to her daughters or any family member about why she seemed to hate her mother. No one understood why she insisted on blaming Maria Antonia for her divorce, a deported lover, and the death of Ricardo Peña.

Since Maria Antonia had recommended a concoction of herbs and teas, she blamed her for Ricardo Peña's death, even though he suffered from gastritis. Later, an autopsy revealed he had died of heart failure.

Growing up, the girls didn't ask their mother pointed questions about abuela. Berating their grandmother was something she would do right out of the blue. They never understood why she blamed her mother for her own mistakes and missteps in life. For example,

> If Toña had not taken me out of school to travel around Texas picking cotton and getting contracts to work in the fields of other states, I would have stayed in school. I could have graduated and maybe even gone to college.

Minerva added, "Toña didn't even listen to my godmother when she asked her to leave me in Dallas with her, instead of taking me to do migratory work." She also told everyone that if her mother had not persuaded her to sell the Dallas home and move to Michigan, she and Manuel López would still be married and living in Dallas, even though she was the one who filed for divorce when Martha López, her second oldest daughter, was two years.

Minerva expressed that "Mercedes was born in Dallas before Manuel went overseas," adding,

> I worked at Braniff Airways and saved enough to buy our first home on Pearl Street. But Toña talked me into selling it and going to Michigan. With her and Beto gone, I'd be

alone in Dallas. There was no guarantee Manuel would return. But I always regretted my decision.

Minerva attributed the break-up of her second relationship to abuela. She explained,

> I would've stayed with Jesús, if Toña had not interfered—he was the only man I ever loved. After he was deported, I'd see him everywhere I went, even in my dreams. Toña never liked him. I think she called los federales to have him deported.

DESPITE MINERVA'S THREATS, Maria Antonia didn't stay away from her oldest grandchildren. After all, she had helped raise them from birth. When Minerva divorced her first husband, she was the surrogate mother to Mercedes and Martha. Her daughter said she didn't need much time to recover from her first failed marriage. Newly divorced, she traveled to Mexico, where she met Jesús Sosa. A subsequent union, unbeknownst to Maria Antonia, brought Anita to Michigan in her mother's womb. The resulting pregnancy prompted her daughter to return to her mother's home until Anita was born.

Minerva obtained prenatal care at a clinic run by the Sisters of Charity, a Roman Catholic order in Saginaw. She had been told her child would not live due to a faint heartbeat and lack of oxygen. In those days, a baby with that diagnosis was called a blue baby, and life expectancy at birth was doubtful.

However, Maria Antonia was fearful for two reasons. On the one hand, Anita's father might come looking for his daughter and take her back to Mexico. In addition, however ill-informed, Maria Antonia believed if immigration authorities caught Jesús Sosa for having entered the country illegally, the newborn was in danger of deportation if she carried his surname. Without honoring her daughter's wishes who was in deep delirium after giving birth,

Maria Antonia took it upon herself to register the new arrival with the López surname just as Minerva's two older daughters. She was relieved when Michigan authorities didn't question her statement concerning the biological father of the newborn.

Minerva's first husband was an American citizen and a veteran. He now lived in New Mexico. Since Minerva had divorced him, Maria Antonia doubted they'd ever see him again. This gave abuelita confidence she had done the best thing for her third granddaughter, Anita, by giving her the surname of López.

Four years after serving in the U.S. Army during World War II, Manuel López returned, hoping to reunite with his wife and daughter. And, while a brief reunion in Dallas produced Martha López, their second child, Minerva divorced him when she was two. She told everyone she never loved him.

When Minerva left a man, she never took him back.

As Anita grew into a young girl much lighter in skin color than her older sisters, she learned more about how she had acquired the surname of López. She also learned why she was affectionately called la güera. Relatives said it was because of her fair skin, hazel eyes and auburn hair. "They always called you the milkman's daughter," abuela would tell Anita. Holding her close, Maria Antonia reminded her "I took care of you from the moment you were born. You were so fair and your eyes so blue that the milkman and the mailman didn't believe I was your grandmother."

Maria Antonia's skin color was as white as any German, Norwegian, Dutch or other northern European. Her neck and torso sported red birthmarks that looked the unmistakable color of natural strawberries. Noticing this unique genetic trait, Anita realized she had inherited some of her grandmother's physical characteristics. Hence, to her, the milkman and mailman story rang true.

Although her grandmother never tired of telling her about the first home she had bought on the outskirts of Saginaw, Anita didn't recall a thing about la casa chiquita, as Maria Antonia called it. While showing her a black-and-white picture of her at age four, abuela would say with a hearty laugh,

91

I used to take you outside when the weather was warm and sunny, and the mailman and the milkman always asked if I was babysitting. When I said you were my granddaughter, they didn't believe me. You were too white, and your eyes were too blue, to be Mexican.

An extremely benevolent soul, Maria Antonia's heart bled for the three little girls left fatherless by her irresponsible daughter. She made them the focus of her life. Mercedes, Martha, and Anita had everything they needed. Religious Catholic holidays, such as Christmas and Easter, were happy for the three girls because of abuela's selfless efforts.

Still, thanks to Maria Antonia's ingenuity, lack of money didn't prevent the family from hanging elaborate decorations on the Christmas tree. Her skillful hands crafted decorations from plain paper or candle holders from discarded bottles. One year, the Christmas tree sported sweet popcorn balls. Since she had been a lifelong seamstress, bits and pieces of cotton, gingham, nylon and the like were always tucked away in baskets waiting to be transformed. In abuelita's hands simple cloth material became rag dolls, doll clothing, curtains, potholders, tablecloths, and other useful items.

Anita looked proudly at her grandmother as she spoke. Abuela's body was so frail that she sometimes imagined it shattering into a thousand pieces, but abuela's mind was still intact. She marveled at how a crisis had brought generations of her grandmother's enormous family together again.

Flanked by wheelchair bound Jeorge on one side, Beto on the other, and her daughter in a front-row seat, abuela continued to talk about the lengthy journey of her life. Unfortunately, many of her grandchildren and great-grandchildren didn't understand. She often said,

This country is made up of nothing but immigrants. We all came looking for a better life than the one we left behind. I still remember that when my husband and I crossed the border with Minerva in my arms and Paco at my side, we were welcomed.

She likened three generations of her progeny as the sprouts that began with her desire to leave Mexico with her husband's complete agreement. Now, in retrospect, and despite his absence, she lived for her retoños—the offshoots. Maria Antonia took pride that her grandchildren and great-grandchildren had produced their own progeny, who in turn, had reproduced many. Reflecting on the past, she added,

> When I look around at all of you, I feel satisfied that you're all the result of my decision to come here. My husband listened to me and together we took that giant step in coming here to escape poverty and tyranny in Mexico. Although he's gone, you are the beneficiaries of our work, our struggles, and our dreams.

Maria Antonia was born on her father's ranch outside of Muzquiz, so she wasn't certain about her age. Using modern technology, a relative had searched for her birth record. He found she had been baptized at a Muzquiz church. The year on the baptismal certificate indicated she was one-hundred and three. Still, Anita had heard she was not a newborn when she was taken into town to be baptized. All these stories Maria Antonia had shared with her descendants.

At her birthday party, Maria Antonia's heartfelt speech was brief and filled with gratitude for her children and the blessings that had been heaped upon the entire clan while in the United States. She thanked the Michigan nursing home staff and said she had never been treated so well.

After an inspiring hour of music from the Mariachi band and a buffet filled with homemade Mexican food—tacos, enchiladas, tamales, and other savory side dishes—Maria Antonia's birthday bash came to a joyful and satisfying end.

Slowly and respectfully, her grandchildren and great-grandchildren hugged and kissed her goodbye. Meanwhile, Hilda helped the nursing home staff gather half eaten plates of food. Pieces of the spectacular birthday cake were divided into wedges and distributed among remaining family members.

After he hugged his mother one last time, Jeorge was wheeled out the door. Beto said he'd return to see her soon. Minerva, who lived with her daughter, Gina Peña Schmidt, the oldest of three from her third marriage, left the nursing home together as soon as the ballroom was clean.

Since there was about an hour left before the mandatory time when all guests had to leave the nursing facility, Maria Antonia looked around at the empty tables and chairs, wondering about the many cards and gifts atop one single table. Hilda and Anita were standing in the nearby doorway, when abuela waved them over anxiously.

She told Hilda, who looked at Anita for a translation, "My room is too small to put up all these gifts. You must take them away and save them." The two granddaughters were left alone with her in the spacious nursing home ballroom.

"I'm feeling too tired to go through all my birthday cards right now. Take them. Save them for me to go through some other day," abuela told Hilda, who, like Anita, felt childlike in front of her grandmother. They obediently complied.

"Don't worry about anything, abuelita. I'll take everything with me to my father's house. In fact, the nursing home director has just approved a visit to his home soon," she said, motioning Anita to translate all that she had said to their grandmother.

"Ante todo, before all else," abuela said,

> Make sure you keep all my birthday cards in a very safe place. They may contain money. You know I have always had a savings account. I will decide how much you can take to the bank for me when I open them. You see, some may even contain a check, which I must sign on the back before you can make the deposit for me.

It had never occurred to either one that their grandmother would care about the many birthday cards she had received. Moreover, they did not think that abuela would care about the money and checks inside each birthday card.

As Hilda stood nearby trying to find space for many gifts of soap, candy, and sleepwear, Anita tucked her grandmother into her assigned twin bed. Because her roommate didn't speak Spanish, Maria Antonia didn't include her. She simply looked up and asked for an extra pillow to tuck under her head.

Anita recalled happier times when she had done the same thing for her loving grandmother in her San Antonio home. After Maria Antonia was safely on her back, Anita would exclaim "patas arriba" or legs up and the two would burst out laughing—they both knew the correct word for legs was piernas.

Tragically, in Texas, abuela was never told that once she became a ward of the state, she lost the right to own any more worldly possessions, including a personal savings account. The state of Texas had even attempted to dispossess her of the San Antonio house.

Anita had talked to Minerva about abuela's forced emergency room visit, and then she called again to say abuelita was being transferred to a San Antonio nursing home. This prompted her mother to board a Greyhound bus to Texas immediately. Having been with abuela when she bought the condemned San Antonio home, Minerva had heard her mother say the house belonged to both. During nearly three decades they had shared the home, Minerva told everyone she would inherit it upon Maria Antonia's death. It took Minerva two days to arrive in Dallas. As soon as Anita picked her up the two headed for San Antonio. As fate would have it, the hospital staff said Maria Antonia had been admitted into a nearby nursing home. After a brief visit, the two went to their property. Anita López had the key to the house so she opened the door. Minerva rushed in and immediately began rummaging through Maria Antonia's possessions, never explaining what she sought.

The possibility abuela would be taken from her home against her own will never occurred to anyone. While disgusted at her mother's reaction to abuela's situation, Anita told Minerva the home was now vacant, adding that she had locked up the house until the crisis was resolved.

The family was unaware that Maria Antonia had hired an attorney to draft a last will and testament, thirty years before Minerva abandoned her. The official will and testament included a power of attorney. That was the sole reason Minerva hurriedly boarded a bus bound for Texas, she had more on her mind than her mother's unexpected predicament.

Anita wanted to believe her mother's cruel words simply reflected her anger against abuela. Anita wanted to believe Minerva would arrive in time to save her. She yearned to see mother and daughter let bygones be bygones. And while she had never seen any physical affection between the two, she hoped to finally see that.

However, back at the dilapidated home, Minerva's actions quickly dashed her hopes for reconciliation between them. Unfamiliar with the court system in Texas and the injustices of the judicial system, Anita could not have guessed her grandmother's life would be turned upside down.

At the hospital at abuela's side, Anita asked Dr. Rudolph Weiss, the attending physician, questions about her grandmother's health. After showing her the results of the x-ray he had taken, the emergency room doctor was candid.

"There is nothing wrong with your grandmother," he emphatically said, confessing,

> The state of Texas Family and Protective Services does this regularly. They send a case worker to an elderly person's home. Then a willing doctor is recruited to conspire with the state to force the elderly into nursing homes. I see this happen all the time.

Anita shouted, causing raised eyebrows and curious looks from the nursing staff and visitors. "That's unbelievable! How can they do that? What can I do to get my grandmother out of here? She doesn't want to be in a nursing home or anywhere else. She wants to die in her own home, doctor."

The doctor replied, "I'm sorry, but there's really nothing emergency room doctors can do. You must go to court and prove she can live alone. As far as her health is concerned, the only thing I see is her high blood pressure." But he asked, "Wouldn't your blood pressure go up if someone came into your home, strapped you to a gurney and forced you into an ambulance?"

Anita broke down hysterically. Doctor Weiss, a tall thin man with horn-rimmed glasses, waved to an orderly to bring a glass of water. She then thanked the doctor for his kind words and never saw him again. After more than an hour in the emergency waiting room, a nurse came and told her that she could finally see her grandmother. Before she could enter a nearby stall with a pair of gray curtains, a portly Hispanic woman donned in business attire approached her.

"My name is Naomi Vasquez and I'm a case worker with the Texas Department of Family and Protective Services." Once she identified herself, the woman said she had left her a voicemail message on the cellular telephone as a courtesy. Now Anita faced the woman who had told her right off in a voicemail that there was nothing she could do. The social worker asked, "Are you the granddaughter who lives in Dallas and has been helping Maria Antonia Menchaca Castañeda?"

Not answering her questions, Anita said,

You said you got a court order from a local judge. You said it allowed you to take my abuelita from her home. Why was a court order necessary? You don't have the right to do that. My grandmother is not sick. She doesn't have Alzheimer's and she wants to stay in her own home!

Anita's blood pressure rose with every word she uttered.

Social worker Vasquez responded, to inform her about their responsibilities for the protection of the elderly:

When the state sees an elderly person is alone and at risk, it mandates intervention. We know Maria Antonia has been living alone for quite some time. We asked a doctor to check her before deciding she needed 24-hour care in a public facility. She has been assigned a court-appointed lawyer who'll serve as her guardian until the case is resolved.

Anita said,

> I believe my grandmother's rights have been violated. Yes, I agree she needed help at times because of her age and disability. Her greatest wish was to remain in her home. Yes, she doesn't speak English very well, but her renters talked to her regularly—all she ever asked for was to die in that old house!

With urgency, abuela's voice called out from behind the gray curtains. She wanted to know who it was.

"Anita, ¿Estás ahí? Anita, "¿Eres tú? Anita, sácame de aquí!"

It was the soft voice of Maria Antonia who recognized Anita and the social worker voices, albeit in English, holding a conversation around her.

Anita didn't wait for further explanations. She entered her space and pulled back one of the curtains. She saw her grandmother lying face up with her tiny feet strapped to stirrups. A hospital bracelet dangled from her right wrist. Anita broke into tears, and Maria Antonia exclaimed in Spanish,

> I'm so happy you are here. Take me out of here. I don't belong here. They came and took me from my home by force. I don't know what they want from me. They've examined me from head to toe, even my panocha vagina has not been spared.

The Spanish word Maria Antonia used to describe how doctors had examined her made Naomi Vasquez and a Hispanic nurse burst out laughing. Maria Antonia didn't flinch at the use of the word, which was taboo among those who spoke polite Spanish.

When Anita found herself alone with abuelita, she explained what had happened. But her grandmother told her to find a way to get her out. As soon as Maria Antonia felt Anita would do as she said, abuelita pulled her granddaughter up close, urging her,

98

You must go back to the house before it's too late. Go to the dresser in my room, the same dresser where you once found money wrapped in old newspapers. Pull out the last drawer and you will find it there.

"Abuelita, you did it again?" Anita said, adding the diminutive "ita" that Spanish speakers use at the end of a name to denote love, intimacy, and affection.

Maria Antonia unheeded Anita's concern, and now more than ever urged her to go back to her south San Antonio home to get the money. Then, she specifically told her to take it to the bank and deposit it in her savings. At the time, no one had told Anita that the state could seize abuelita's property. She suppressed her feelings— didn't have the heart to tell Maria Antonia what the emergency doctor had told her about the nursing home. Nevertheless, as abuela laid in the hospital bed, unable to escape, Maria Antonia continued to argue that there was no reason for her hospitalization.

Anita wondered if abuelita had known all along about Texas' ploy to commit her to an elderly nursing home. There were numerous times she had implored her grandmother to visit a doctor and she had always resisted. Anita recalled that one summer abuela nearly had a heart attack when the temperature rose to 102-degrees—there was no air conditioning and she only relied on a floor fan to cool the hot summers. When the ambulance arrived, abuela refused to be taken to a hospital.

She now knew why her grandmother had always resisted doctors' visits and any mention of hospitalization. She had once told Anita about a friend who'd been forced into a nursing home, after an ambulance had taken her to a hospital. Anita reasoned, Maria Antonia had cause to fear a doctor's visit, an ambulance, a hospital, or calls from social services.

While she was at the hospital, Anita's cellphone rang. It was Gina Peña Schmidt who called Anita to inform her that Minerva had taken a Texas bound bus and asked her to pick up Minerva at the Dallas bus station. Unaware that Maria Antonia had been transferred to a nursing home, mother and daughter drove to San Antonio.

Anita pondered getting her grandmother out of the nursing home and back into her home. All her property taxes and utilities were current. Her renters, who had stood by tearfully unable to rescue her from being strapped to a gurney, were unable to stop her hospitalization. Anita did not realize that despite her grandmother's responsible track record, the state would now determine her fate.

Once Anita assured her grandmother that she would do everything possible to get her out, she kissed abuelita's forehead and said goodbye. Blinded by tears over what had happened to her grandmother, Anita had trouble driving. Still, at breakneck speed, she drove to the Dallas downtown Greyhound bus station. Deep inside her mind, Anita swore she would never forgive herself for trusting public services. If she had not asked for help, abuelita would still be in her old home feeding the birds and squirrels that visited her two-story backyard deck. Had she not called Meals on Wheels, maybe fewer city agencies would've known Maria Antonia lived alone. Anita cried and agonized over her decision to seek help for her grandmother. But she lived so far away. She couldn't always be there to ensure her grandmother was fed, washed and, and most of all, safe. The part that most bothered Anita was that there was absolutely nothing wrong with abuela's memory. Yes. She was very, very old. But she was perfectly aware of her surroundings, and, although she hobbled down the stairs to collect the rent from her inquilinos, she did it. They loved her for it. The inquilinos were content because she kept track of her electric, water, and phone bills—she was never late. As well, when there was a maintenance problem with the house, abuela either had the money stashed aside or had budgeted it for the anticipated expense. On the other hand, the spendthrift, Minerva's social security check instantly disappeared and she never contributed to the household.

Anita knew her grandmother's exceptional memory-maintained remnants of the Mexican Revolution. She knew from many conversations with Maria Antonia that the United States had discriminated against Mexicans as much as it had the "Negro," an acceptable term before the 1964 Civil Rights Act.

Thanks to Maria Antonia, Anita had learned both American and Mexican history. Abuela spoke about their mistreatments. "When we walked into a store to buy food, Anglos would look down on us. We wore blue jeans because so often we worked as fieldhands. And look at Anglos today; they wear blue jeans daily," she would exclaim, clarifying that she had raised her four children to be proud, honest, hard-working citizens of the United States.

Anita had hoped that when her mother arrived, Minerva would get abuela released, as abuelita could not be held more than 24 hours. Minerva's arrival reminded Anita that over the years, abuela's three grown sons had visited her in Texas with their wives and children. Along with Maria Antonia, Minerva usually hosted her brothers. Anita, however, had lost contact with her entire family over a period of nearly thirty years. That's why she was little more than a stranger when Jeorge, dispatched his only son, George Castañeda Jr. and his sister, Hilda, to investigate abuela' discharge.

AFTER THE BIRTHDAY PARTY, watching Hilda gather her grandmother's gifts and cards, Anita mused about how much Maria Antonia's life had changed. As they wheeled her to her room, neither one was going to tell her she had been stripped of all her possessions and rights, including the right to have a personal savings account. Maria Antonia told her granddaughters, as they returned to her room,

> Now make sure you don't lose my birthday cards, because if they contain money, I want to have a savings account in Michigan. You know I don't like being without a savings account. You never know what emergency will arise. You should never be without money!

Her children and grandchildren would soon learn that under Texas law, removing an elderly person from her own home under the guise of neglect and for her health and safety meant taking home, property, personal belongings, and bank accounts from them.

Additionally, in its distorted wisdom, the court chose a temporary guardian that was non-Spanish speaking. How could this have happened? Anita López thought. Her grandmother had always talked about passing away in her home. Explaining this to a court-appointed attorney was to no avail. The attorney merely said the alternative was to go to court and let a judge decide Maria Antonia's fate.

Once the state of Texas stepped in, the relative or guardian would have to prove they had cared about the person in question. Minerva's absence led to Maria Antonia's forced removal from her home. Although it took time, the family's attorney would succeed in having her transferred to Michigan.

The conditions under which her grandmother lived were no laughing matter. The mattress on which Maria Antonia slept was so worn out that it sank under her weight. Nonetheless, any attempt to replace it was met with loud protests by Maria Antonia. She saw her 1940s furniture, carefully assembled in her living room, as elegant. There was no need to replace it. A vintage Singer sewing machine doubled as a desk, when Maria Antonia was not busy making an apron or sewing a garment. A metal kitchen chair doubled as a walker or walking cane.

Over the years, Anita had learned that physical suffering did not seem to faze her grandmother. To be sure, Maria Antonia's poor living conditions disturbed those who loved her. Unfortunately, Maria Antonia had always rejected offers to improve her surroundings. Pride had prevailed in old age as it had in her youth.

From the outset, the awkward-leaning house Maria Antonia had bought with cash and her life savings barely met basic living standards. But hardships, such as freezing cold spells in the winter and infernos in the summer, only strengthened her resolve to hang on to her San Antonio home. Beto was a handy man. He had fixed heating and plumbing problems on summer vacations in Texas. Maria Antonia's youngest son was the most jovial. He was too young to be drafted during World War II and the Korean War, so she had depended on him for many things.

Her other son, Paco lived in Peoria, Illinois after the war. He seldom visited his family. And when he did, Maria Antonia would end up in tears. In later years, Paco continued visiting Michigan but spoke only to his siblings. Years later, he and his family visited Maria Antonia once during the many years she lived in San Antonio.

Jeorge and his wife visited every summer. The conditions she lived in prompted them to go food shopping for Maria Antonia. The couple always said her refrigerator was empty. She said that wasn't true. "They just want to make up for throwing me out of their home," she would say. Jeorge was a no-nonsense kind of a man who seldom smiled. He spoke so loudly in normal conversations that Anita thought he was perpetually belligerent. Years later, she found out he had been forced to speak loudly while working at the General Motors plant in Saginaw. Noisy machines surrounded blue-collar workers forcing them to scream at one another to communicate. Jeorge told his sister one day,

> She tells people we threw her out of our new home, but that isn't true. My mother was always a very proud woman. She worked hard and she worked us hard in the fields. But when I bought the ten-acre parcel to build our home, I didn't expect my family to work like fieldhands and migrants.

His only interest was to see his hard-working mother rest. Jeorge added that he wanted her to "take it easy for the first time in her life. And instead, mother got mad when I told her neither she nor my family had to work so hard; they are not migrant workers!" Still, when visiting, he did his best to help his mother improve her train-wrecked San Antonio home. He went to hardware stores and brought back screens so she could open her windows during the hot Texas summers. He bought space heaters for the bone-chilling weather. Minerva had tried to insulate it, installing pieces of pink insulation purchased at a local hardware store. The two women froze during the winter months. Still, in the summer months, the old rickety house was unbearably hot. Space heaters in the winter and fans in the summer helped the mother and daughter survive for years. Despite the horrible conditions, which kept Michigan family members wondering how the two women survived, Maria Antonia staunchly defended her decision to buy the house situated less than a mile from the old San José Spanish mission.

Indeed, she proudly stated she and her daughter would never be "arrimadas" or beholden to family members, if they had their own home. Neither one ever talked about a last will and testament. So as far as the family knew, there was no formal document or estate beneficiary.

While Maria Antonia's dire situation had forced her daughter to return to Texas, she had primarily returned to claim the house the two had shared. Since Anita didn't know about the will, she couldn't understand why the first thing Minerva did was to rummage through Maria Antonia's boxes.

The one and only time she returned to visit; Minerva had taken copies of certificates showing Maria Antonia had stock in General Motors worth some nine hundred dollars. When Maria Antonia discovered the missing certificates, all she could say was her daughter might've needed the money more than she did. She told her granddaughter there was no need to ask if she had cashed them. After all, she was listed as the beneficiary on the certificates. That's why Anita López didn't understand what she was looking for, as she went on a rampage through abuelita's bedroom. She had already cashed in her grandmother's General Motors stock certificates. So, what else could she be looking for so desperately? Anita wondered.

Through some miracle, the only personal items that escaped her rampage were the yellow, battered letters Jeorge Castañeda had written to his mother during the war. Maria Antonia had tied them up neatly with a big yellow ribbon and placed them inside a black patent leather purse.

Anita and her cousins didn't know that when an elderly person is taken from their home by the state of Texas, their home is confiscated, and their bank accounts are frozen. Unaware of Texas law, Minerva immediately put the house up for sale.

When the court discovered Maria Antonia's living conditions, they blamed her daughter, because she had abandoned her mother. Consequently, Minerva would not be allowed to become her mother's guardian, nor would the court allow her any claims to the real estate property. Suddenly, Minerva shouted in response to Anita's question regarding her ransacking of Maria Antonia's house.

That house is mine! Toña always said I would inherit it when she died. In fact, I was the one who found the house. We had been renting another old house nearby, but she and I wanted a house of our own.

Minerva had always done exactly as she had pleased throughout her life. Her thinking was erratic and unorthodox. She felt completely justified in selling the house before the Family and Protective Services intervened. However, rather than sell the house outright through a realtor, she offered the home to friends and sold it through a contract executed by a local San Antonio bank, for $45,900 dollars. Without giving anyone notice, Minerva sold the home, and kept the sale secret from Anita, her cousins, their father, and more importantly, Maria Antonia, while they were battling the Texas courts on her behalf. What most mattered to the three cousins was that they simply wanted to save their grandmother from confinement in the San Antonio nursing home where she had been placed against her own will.

On the day in which Hilda was granted guardianship, the judge asked to hear from Minerva. She was nowhere to be found. When asked about her whereabouts the young lawyer representing the three grandchildren had nothing to say. As was her pattern, Minerva had not considered her mother's situation or stayed to hear the judge's decision, she simply drew papers on the house and fled to Michigan.

The judge threatened to hold the attorney in contempt of court if he did not return to explain Minerva's whereabouts. The attorney would later reveal that Minerva had sold the house and boarded a bus to Michigan. The court held Minerva responsible for the illegal disposition of Maria Antonia's estate.

Anita had more serious concerns, imagining that if Maria Antonia remained in San Antonio, whether in her home or in the nursing home, she would die without anyone at her bedside. She was the only relative in Texas. That's why, after years of having her grandmother only hours away, Anita reluctantly agreed that the best thing was to transfer her to be near family.

After the judge verified all the facts, he granted Hilda guardianship of Maria Antonia. Nevertheless, the judge required abuelita to be transferred to a licensed twenty-four-hour a day facility in Michigan, where she could be near her adult children, grandchildren, and great-grandchildren.

George Jr., Hilda, and Anita breathed a collective sigh of relief. They had succeeded in saving their grandmother from certain premature death at a San Antonio nursing home. As soon as the judge ended the hearing, a sense of relief filled the threesome. The cousins hurriedly headed to the nursing home. Anita was gripped by fear that the judge would change her mind and force abuelita to remain in San Antonio indefinitely, and what most frightened her was that her unpredictable mother would show up and cause a stir in the courtroom.

As Anita drove the rented red Toyota to the nursing home, her cousins spoke about the fear they experienced during the court proceedings. They laughed as they recalled the look on their attorney's face, when he was nearly held in contempt of court through no fault of his own, just for not knowing the whereabouts of Minerva who had ignored an order to appear.

Since they began fighting to have their grandmother transferred to Michigan, the three cousins spoke about having learned much about the Texas justice system. For instance, from the moment Maria Antonia was strapped to a gurney she'd lost her civil rights—rights guaranteed by the United States Constitution. Because Anita had locked abuelita's home while she waited for her mother to arrive, the Texas Department of Family Services could not seize her home, and Minerva would not have sold it. When Maria Antonia was appointed a lawyer who didn't speak Spanish, the court denied her the right to understand the proceedings, and if the emergency room doctor had testified, he would've had to repeat what he told Anita—that her grandmother was in perfect health. Then, the outcome could have been different.

When Anita pulled into the nursing home parking lot, she had to restrain herself from leaping through the front door to tell the interim director that the court had granted their grandmother's transfer. Rather than sprinting with joy down the hall to her grandmother's tiny room, Anita surprised abuela with the explanation that she would be released. Maria Antonia didn't resist and began pushing her wheelchair toward the exit. Anita couldn't help but feel they had rescued her from a premature death.

As she walked toward abuela, Anita told herself "Walk fast but don't run especially while pushing the wheelchair." This was not a dream. The judge granted a transfer so abuela could be closer to her family in Michigan.

Victorious the cousins left the courtroom together.

During the weeks Maria Antonia had been a nursing home resident, she had observed the unhealthy conditions and unprofessional treatment of dozens of elderly folks. So as painful as it was to put her grandmother on an airplane bound for Michigan, the three cousins agreed it was best for her. Maria Antonia had fended for herself during the years she had lived alone, certain she would die in her own home. Although she had difficulty walking, thinking of her home as her final resting place was what kept her going. She had always rejected wheelchairs, opting for a chair she pushed around from room to room. Her only real issue was arthritis in her hands and knees, which she treated with Tylenol.

Talking to anyone and no one at the same time, Maria Antonia said, "Anita, vuelve mañana," Maria Antonia said as she closed her eyes. Anita said she would return tomorrow to visit. During the years she'd traveled by airplane to Michigan to see her grandmother she had realized how lucky she was to have a grandmother like Maria Antonia.

"¡Te quiero abuelita!" The words of love in Spanish seemed to hold much more meaning than when uttered in English, she thought. "Sí, volveré mañana." Anita promised to return the next day, as she backed away from her grandmother's bedside. Hilda, quiet by nature, simply smiled and followed close behind.

Her descendants were happy to have abuelita back. All agreed that Michigan was good for her.

As many other times, the final birthday party in honor of Maria Antonia Menchaca had been a resounding success. All her children and their progeny had attended. Nieces and nephews and friends had rounded out the huge celebration. The letter from President George W. Bush and First Lady Laura Bush was "the icing on the cake," and had impressed everyone.

Hilda and Anita were grateful to a friend who had come up with the idea to request the special birthday greeting from the White House. Nobody could've imagined Maria Antonia would've questioned the letter's authenticity. In retrospect, Anita López could have predicted it. Over the years, she had listened to her sermons on a variety of issues. In fact, she thought that if Maria Antonia had had a formal education, she might've been an attorney or even a judge. "La gente miente diciendo que soy bruja. People lie when they say I'm a witch," Maria Antonia would say. Then she would exclaim, "¿Dónde está la prueba? Where is the proof?" She commented, knowing her own daughter had started the rumor everyone found unbelievable.

Although she would confront Minerva about her lies occasionally, Maria Antonia felt her daughter lent a deaf ear to her denials about being a witch. Nevertheless, she would proceed to explain that in Mexico they had ancient Indian customs of using herbs as natural medicine. Indigenous people used a variety of plants and flowers in medicine and cooking. They also used them to heal physical ailments: "Como entonces no había doctores. Since there were no doctors back then," Maria Antonia said in Spanish. "When you girls were very sick as babies, I told Minerva about some of the teas that would help you get well. And when her daughter Gina was born with a twisted arm, I suggested a "curandero" to help her. She clarified, "Doctors wanted to operate but el curandero healed and straightened out her little arm."

One unsavory topic repeated for many years was that it was Maria Antonia's fault that Paco, her only Mexican-born son, had gotten into trouble with the United States Immigration and Naturalization Service. When he learned to drive, he wanted to go to Mexico to visit his father. She desired to see her own family as well. So, Paco drove them to Mexico in a used truck that was paid with cash.

In Muzquiz, they found Manuel Castañeda alive and living with his oldest biological son. When Maria Antonia finally heard that his son, Juan, had persuaded Manuel to return to Mexico, Maria Antonia became enraged, and blamed Manuel for depriving her own children from having a father. As for Manuel, she insisted he should've remained with her because the children they had had together were younger and needed him more than his older children in Mexico. Armed with that conviction, Maria Antonia never forgave Manuel, nor did she ever reunite with him.

Maria Antonia and her husband were Catholic. After their youngest son Gilberto, who would be known as Beto was born, abuelita insisted on separate beds. This physical distance may have been the reason Manuel returned to Mexico, when Beto was a child.

Even at the birthday, conflict among Maria Antonia and Minerva could spark at any moment. For example, rumors linking her mother to witchcraft could instantaneously explode. Minerva forcefully denied being the one that spread rumors about her own mother. The baseless tale that she had dabbled in witchcraft was never believed by anyone. Maria Antonia's granddaughters had always asked her to stop. But the unjust rumors continued throughout Maria Antonia's life.

Minerva was an infant when Maria Antonia and her husband entered the United States. She had not grown up knowing about the famous "curanderas" as her mother had. These "healers" generally used a host of flowers, herbs, and teas as purported cures for most any ailment. Not surprisingly, Maria Antonia had learned much about natural cures from Juana Vega. Small towns in Mexico were full of people who used home remedies to cure all maladies. And it was not unusual to do things, such as put a cup of turtle oil under the crib of a sick child to ward off disease or tie a thread around a finger that may have sprouted warts.

Once again, as Maria Antonia repeatedly told everyone: "Anyone can make an accusation against another person. But ask them to show you proof and you'll see how quickly the accusations die." Proof or no proof, she didn't hold a grudge against her daughter for spreading unfounded rumors and lies. She had fought false accusations before.

One day when her children were busy doing the backbreaking work of picking strawberries with her in Ohio, she was attacked. A woman rushed at her wielding a rake and accused her of stealing one of her bushels. Maria Antonia was not afraid of her—never afraid of anything or anyone. She just didn't think a bushel of strawberries was worth fighting for. After all, most migrants earned as little as forty cents an hour, and more often they were paid according to the number of tiny baskets they filled. Despite Maria Antonia's efforts to calm the woman, she continued to call her a thief and began to scream at her, saying migrants didn't get the minimum wage or unemployment benefits. So, the pittance of forty cents per bushel for picking strawberries was all they had. With that, she lunged at Maria Antonia.

When other fieldhands heard the arguing, they stopped what they were doing and rushed over to see why the two women were shouting at one another, hands raised and poised to throw a possible punch or two. Maria Antonia told Anita about the incident.

> We ended up pulling each other's hair in the middle of the field. The men gathered around and laughed until they cried. I was not going to stand still and let someone accuse me of stealing. No señor, all my life I've worked and never have I taken what was not mine or what I did not earn.

Respect for the American flag and patriotism were also values this poor, Mexican immigrant grandmother had passed on to her grandchildren. One day, when Anita and Martha were still in grade school, their mother allowed them to visit their abuelita. The girls were watching Maria Antonia make their favorite Mexican pastry, sweet-potato-filled empanadas. She looked out her second-story kitchen window and spied two teenage boys dragging the American flag through the street. Promptly, she stopped rolling the dough, cleaned her hands, and hurried down a flight of stairs with the girls in tow to stop them. Abuela said, "Sabes ¿Cómo se dice bandera? How do you say flag in English?" To her granddaughters, she repeated, "You, sabe soldados fight for you. Mis hijos fueron a la guerra por este país. My sons fought for this country." Her aim was to impart that they should respect the flag and their country.

The boys' faces spoke volumes. Here was a non-English speaking immigrant who cared enough to teach them to respect the American flag and its significance. This was a lesson the boys would not forget. For years to come, Anita and her sister said that that was the day they learned all about patriotism. Although Minerva was too stubborn to admit it, her mother also had instilled the spirit of patriotism in her. This was reflected during the time she spent teaching theater arts to the children of Mexican immigrants in the small Michigan town.

Saginaw's Mexican community center was the scene of many plays depicting the creation of the American flag by Betsy Ross and recitations of the American Constitution and its Bill of Rights. Young children of immigrants performed theater while simultaneously learning American history, thanks to Minerva.

THE LIFELONG WEDGE between Maria Antonia and Paco can be attributed to her empathy for others. Not realizing the seriousness of helping someone into the U.S. illegally, Maria Antonia had allowed an old friend to hide in the back of a pickup truck driven by young Paco.

Maria Antonia owned a taco cafe in Laredo prior to entering the United States. During her time as a business owner, she came across Belén Ortega, recognizing her instantly from her wide brown face, bushy eyebrows, and raspy voice. Belén had been wounded while serving as a soldadera in Mexico's Revolution and was crippled from wounds she suffered in battle. Her raven hair was now gray and her cinnamon-colored face bore deep scars. Maria Antonia took pity on the half-starved woman and their friendship flourished.

This poor, spiritually and physically broken woman had saved her and her father from Pancho Villa's followers. Maria Antonia felt a deep sense of gratitude for the woman's brave intervention and looked beyond her physical appearance. During the bloody revolution it was common for Pancho Villa or the federalists to go through a northern Mexico town wreaking havoc. She had survived those fiery rides that instilled fear and panic in the poor villagers, stifling government support in favor of la revolución and the spirit of nationalism.

In the 1930s, Paco drove his mother to Muzquiz in their pickup truck. A chance encounter with Belén Ortega led Maria Antonia to hide her in the back of the truck to get entry into the U.S. She allowed this unlawful request when she saw her rescuer begging at the border. Mexico had not improved with the revolution.

Maria Antonia and her husband had entered the United States months before the Immigration Act of 1924 was enacted. As far as Maria Antonia knew, entering the U.S. without documents was still merely trespassing. This transgression was in no way an official crime, much less a felony, she thought.

Belén Ortega had a sister in Goliad, and she wanted to join her. When border agents found her hiding in the truck, Paco Castañeda was arrested. While the women were released within a day, Paco spent several days in jail and almost lost his green card. Then, trespassing was a misdemeanor. If he had committed a crime, he would not have been accepted into the U.S. Army. But that's what happened in 1942. Later, the family learned he had changed his surname to avoid the stigma of having been jailed and to escape future legal entanglements.

Despite the ordeal, he was proud of being a World War II and Korea veteran. Like his brother, Paco had been wounded in action and received a Purple Heart for their bravery. Maria Antonia was proud of her sons. Yet Paco never forgave her for putting him in a situation that landed him in jail. In the 1940s, Paco married a woman from Illinois. The family heard what had happened to him each time he visited Michigan. More tragic than having been jailed was that he would never be known as Francisco Menchaca Castañeda.

Conversations about the family's history was bound to surface at any time. At Maria Antonia's welcome home celebration, the family found out that Beto told his mother that Paco had died two years earlier. That might have been the reason Maria Antonia had not asked about him at the nursing home. When he died, Maria Antonia was still in her San Antonio home. Anita knew but had not told her, fearing a shock would kill her instantly. The family was reluctant to tell Maria Antonia, however, to everyone's surprise, Beto had no qualms about telling her.

Maybe it was the throng of relatives and friends, or the Mariachi music, or the elaborate cake, or the happiness of seeing her long-lost cousin, Melecio Menchaca, that made Maria Antonia not notice her son's absence. Whatever the reason, everyone agreed the party had been a rousing success. When the mass of relatives and friends had finally left, Hilda and Anita seized the opportunity to talk about Maria Antonia's Texas "estate" and how its sale would help with the inevitable funeral expenses. No one knew that Minerva had sold it.

Anita felt sad knowing she'd only be able to visit her grandmother once a year now that she was in Michigan. On her flight back, Anita didn't dwell on the future but instead resolved to spend each precious moment with abuelita.

The following morning, Anita returned to the Frankenmuth nursing home, arriving right after residents had finished breakfast. Maria Antonia was seated in her wheelchair at a table across from two other residents. She was wiping her mouth with a napkin, when she saw her granddaughter.

A childish happy giggle escaped Maria Antonia' lips, as she told Anita,

I'm so happy you've come back. I want you to stay all day so we can talk. I am getting used to my new home. But I don't have anyone to talk to. Nobody here speaks Spanish. At least in my home the inquilinos would come and talk to me when they paid the rent.

Anita López expressed that the lack of Spanish speakers made her feel alienated and told abuelita, "I'll be sure to talk to Hilda and to the director about that." Unlike the San Antonio nursing home, this home didn't have any Spanish-speaking residents. Still, a professional staff, who tried to communicate with her using sign language, was a great comfort to the whole family.

Anita calmed her grandmother down by pointing out that all three of her children lived nearby and spoke Spanish fluently. She also reminded her that their wives also spoke Spanish. She told her that they too would visit sometime and speak Spanish to her.

Unfortunately, the many grandchildren and great-grandchildren now close enough to visit would not be able to communicate because they only spoke English. They would probably never get to know Maria Antonia's wit, wisdom, and unique gestures, the way Anita had. Abuela listened to what she said but preferred to engage her in conversation for hours on end. Still recalling what had happened in San Antonio, abuela didn't launch into her usual storytelling. The thought that dominated her mind focused on what was going to happen to her home.

"Did you buy a big lock for the front door?" Abuela asked Anita, telling her in Spanish,

> I don't understand why your mother left Texas and came here. It's her home as much as it is mine. But she needs to keep it locked until I get back. Then we can live together again, if she'll stay.

Abuela's sweet gaze made Anita wither with guilt. How was she going to make abuela understand that she was never going to see her San Antonio home again? How could she explain that Minerva had sold her home on a contract basis to one of Maria Antonia's inquilinos or renters? Then, guessing that she might be looking for money, Anita told Minerva,

> Mom, I need to tell you that abuelita had a will and testament drawn up while you were living in Michigan. Because I've been helping her for the past five years, mak-

ing sure she had food and paying her bills, she made me the beneficiary.

Enraged, to hear that. Minerva screamed, "You don't have any right! That testament is no good! I have a power of attorney and that house is mine! Do you hear me? And I can sell it." She hollered at Anita. Angered by the news that her mother had hired a lawyer to draw up a new will, Minerva could not believe she had been excluded as beneficiary.

Anita was only helping abuela, given her health and circumstance, thus Anita shouted at Minerva,

> I don't want this house. I have my own home. I'd never take it from you. But you left abuelita alone. She gave you money to pay for her burial plot. But you didn't do it. I didn't want her buried in a pauper's grave. That was the reason I agreed to the new will.

Anita didn't know a formal will had been drawn up by Minerva and her abuela, when she took Maria Antonia to a lawyer to draw up a new one. The legal matter took place near the old San Antonio courthouse at her lawyer's office. The attorney's staff acted as witnesses at the signing of the new will.

The attorney doubted Maria Antonia's sanity, so he asked her if she realized she was excluding her own children in favor of her granddaughter. It was one of the few occasions Anita witnessed her strong character. Maria Antonia rose slowly with help from her granddaughter. She looked the lawyer right in the eye, and firmly told him, in Spanish,

> My daughter, Minerva, abandoned me several years ago. My sons in Michigan have nothing to do with this house. I bought it with my own savings so that my daughter and I would never need to be 'arrimadas' beholden in the homes of my sons or anyone else.

Maria Antonia told the attorney, who blushed with embarrassment for doubting her judgment and her sanity. She continued,

Minerva, my only daughter, left me years ago. The only person who has taken the time to help me has been my Anita. I don't want to be a burden to her or any of my family when I die. I want Anita to have the house so she can sell it and pay for my funeral.

That was the last time the two visited the attorney. After that, Anita registered the will in the San Antonio de Bexar County courthouse and forgot about it. Her mother's mysterious ransacking of the house, while Maria Antonia languished in a nursing home, prompted Anita to remember. When Minerva revealed she was the beneficiary in a will drawn up years earlier, Minerva insisted any other will was void. Anita knew the most current one would prevail in a Texas court. But she did not have the heart to challenge her mother. She did not want to engage in legal battle over an old house that was dangerously tilting to the left.

Anxious to please her mother, Anita listened calmly as Minerva mulled selling the house. It had suddenly become hot property. The historic Mission San José, albeit neglected for years, was now being renovated. The goal was to attract more tourism to poor, mainly Hispanic, south San Antonio. Mission San Antonio de Valero, commonly known as the Alamo, never lacked investment. It had been showered with financial support since the 1900s. However, Mission San Jose was one of four missions on the poor side of town and the mission suffered from as much neglect, as Maria Antonia's broken-down home on Roosevelt Avenue.

San Jose Mission, Mission Concepción, Mission San Juan, and Mission Espada—all missions south of the Alamo. When Maria Antonia and Minerva lived in the house, the missions had not yet been declared World Heritage Sites by the United Nations Education, Science, and Cultural Organization.

At seventy, Minerva had become a religious zealot and focused on saving her soul. She was no longer interested in home-made potions aimed at preserving her face and body. Her last and final boyfriend, twenty years her junior, was no longer a romantic interest.

Maria Antonia had raised Minerva as a Catholic, but she had long ago left the church. After stints as a Pentecost, Nazarene, and a Rosicrucian, Minerva spent her time talking about the Bible and quoting scripture. She felt it was now her duty to evangelize. She talked incessantly about evil human weakness and frailty. "Nowadays, the devil is on the loose. Look at all the horrible things happening in the world today. Jesus is our savior, and we should pray and read the Bible every day." Then, after that rapid-fire quoting of a scripture, she'd ask Anita, "Do you go to church?" Also, she even took to asking her each time if she had repented.

Anita looked at her mother in dismay when she spoke about Jesus and forgiveness. She would never admit she didn't practice what she preached regarding her mother. And this attitude enraged her daughter.

Anita cried angrily, while Minerva just shook her head in total denial, telling her mother, "How could you leave abuelita all alone? You knew she couldn't walk; you knew she was deaf; you knew she had rheumatoid arthritis, and you knew she didn't speak enough English to defend herself in case of an emergency."

Although she had three children and several grandchildren in Michigan, Minerva didn't want to return. But she feared a neighbor would report her to the city's family court, which had allowed her to adopt the boy, Francisco, even though she was physically unable to raise a child at her advanced age. Minerva had argued that the newborn's mother and grandmother were both unfit to raise the child. Both women consumed drugs and alcohol. Compassion led her to adopt the boy. But a neighbor threatened to have the boy taken away. That's when Minerva Castañeda Peña devised a plan to leave Texas. She did not care about leaving Maria Antonia then ninety-eight years old to fend for herself, and she convinced Maria Antonia to withdraw her entire life savings to buy a 1978 Buick from a local we-tote-the-note dealership. Anita begged her abuelita not to do it. Minerva told her that hauling groceries home on a bus with an unruly child required a car.

Maria Antonia believed her and approved a withdrawal of $6,500 dollars, which Anita witnessed when she drove her to the bank. A few days later, Minerva packed up the Buick and strapped the boy to a car seat and left for Michigan.

Now, five years after abandoning her mother, Minerva sold the house to people who had been renting from Maria Antonia. Bible-toting born again Christians, the buyers promised to convert the tiny house in the backyard to a chapel, as Minerva requested. With that stipulation, Minerva sold them the house on a ten-year contract. The home buyer was an undocumented immigrant from Mexico who paid religiously for the first two years. The third year of the contract the main buyer was deported, leaving his two sisters to continue paying for the home on a payment plan. Yet, Maria Antonia didn't know her daughter had sold her home until the last year of her residency in Frankenmuth. By then, she and Minerva had buried the hatchet and begun trying to focus on forgiveness.

Mother and daughter had lived in the dilapidated San Antonio home for nearly thirty years. Although Anita had visited for many years, she had no desire to own such a property on the seedy side of town. And the home's precarious bent always invited comments as to its safety.

Maria Antonia had been warned that the house might topple any day. But she always replied by offering her critics a bite to eat, even perfect strangers who knocked on her door. Once they accepted, she would either quiz them or offer her insight on various and sundry topics.

Vicente Mas was one of the most outspoken critics. While she beguiled him with her stories, he worried about the home's foundation and its need of repairs. On occasion, he accompanied his wife, Anita, to see how both women were doing. While he enjoyed visiting, Vicente was no match for Maria Antonia's wit and wisdom. She didn't hesitate telling Vicente Mas what she thought, as he sat eating her delicious carne guisada, flour tortillas, and cumin-infused rice.

Do you really think my old house is going to fall? My house was built 100 years ago, and it is constructed better than today's modern homes. Homes today are just made from cardboard. My home is so sturdy and solid it could withstand an earthquake.

Maria Antonia would speak about the high ceilings, the solid wooden window frames and doors, and pointing to the wood flooring, she told Vicente that she never had to take shelter because of flooding around the San Antonio River. Vicente noticed Maria Antonia always had a story to tell while talking about the virtues of her old house. He also noted that over the years, he'd grown accustomed to her thought-provoking riddles. He said she had devised the riddles so that regardless of a person's intelligence, only she had the correct answer. Of course, this trait along with her generosity and hospitality had endeared her to him.

Now, as Anita watched Maria Antonia go into a deep sleep, Anita recalled the many times she had tossed stones from the driveway at her second-floor bedroom windows to wake her up. Even if she called to let her grandmother know she was driving down from Dallas for a monthly visit, Anita regularly found her grandmother sound asleep. In Anita's mind, her grandmother was the very salt of the earth. Time and again she had seen abuelita come to the rescue of someone in need. For instance, Anita remembered that one time one of the renters could not afford to have a tooth pulled. Instead of collecting the rent from her, Maria Antonia offered to pay the dentist.

Her acts of kindness throughout her life had endeared her to many family members and renters of her first-floor apartments. As well, total strangers had benefitted from her compassion. Stray dogs and cats, even squirrels and birds, all knew of her kindness because she fed them daily.

One of her inquilinos was a young Mexican woman with two children. Her husband worked in construction in and around San Antonio. But the couple still struggled to pay Maria Antonia the $45 a week for the two-bedroom apartment on the ground floor. Then, one day when a tenant climbed the flight of stairs to say that she couldn't pay the rent on time, Maria Antonia asked her why she looked so distraught. The renter confessed she had lost much sleep due to an excruciatingly painful toothache. Without a word, Maria Antonia stood up and pushed her chair to retrieve a handful of dollar bills. When she returned to give them to the young mother, she refused to accept it. Maria Antonia insisted and compassionately told her,

> All of us need help at one time or another. Many of us struggle to earn money to feed the family and keep a roof over our heads. I know you and your husband are hard working. So, you must accept this. No te preocupes. Don't worry just call it a loan you will repay when you can.

Anita, her cousins, and the rest of the family had hoped Maria Antonia's return to Michigan as a nursing home resident would restore the trust and love between her children and her. Minerva knew the most details about her mother's life. Beto still wanted answers. Now a retiree, he was the one in the family who found time to visit his mother daily. He seemed to be searching for the truth about why he had never known his father. He wondered why his mother had never tried to reunite with him, so he asked. "¿Por qué no te reuniste con mi papa? Yo nunca conocí a mi papa. ¿Por qué no fuiste a buscarlo?"

Instead of answering her youngest child's questions, Maria Antonia would run her wrinkled hand over his face and tell him how much she loved him. Then she'd go into her Spanish ancestry and explain that it was the reason he was born with dishwater blond hair and green eyes.

Although Beto had married a Mexican woman whose family reflected a dark Mexican with brown skin stereotype, the couple had produced two beautiful daughters with eyes as green as precious emeralds. Beto was the image of his grandfather's Spanish heritage, as his only son mirrored the Indigenous in them.

The only time Maria Antonia returned to Mexico was with Paco. She visited her father's grave. Aunts Teofela and Enriqueta had died. The home where she had grown up was gone. But the church where she had been baptized was still there, so she and her son talked to a priest about her aunts and family members. To Maria Antonia's astonishment, the aging priest ushered her into a storage area in the sacristy where he pointed to the baúl trunk her father had deposited there many years earlier. The priest told her that he had left the baúl with him on one of his many visits to see her and her aunts. With Paco at her side, Maria Antonia took the rusty key from the priest and opened the mysterious chest.

Just as Roque Menchaca had once told Maria Antonia, the baúl contained a Bible and old documents. The papers were official legal documents that conferred ownership of the farm and acreage to her family. This was fortunate because in Mexico, without legal title, Mexicans could not claim any land as their own. Peasants toiled for generations on land they were prevented from owning. Benito Juarez had tried to improve conditions after Mexico's Independence from Spain. The Menchaca family was among a handful of Mexicans who apparently had clear title to their lands prior to the Porfirio Diaz regime.

Maria Antonia would never deny or feel shame about her maternal Indigenous heritage, but her father's love and influence continued to fill her with pride as an adult. Pride and respect prompted her to make sure she retrieved her father's old trunk when she and Paco drove to Muzquiz, Mexico.

When she and Belén were released after Paco was arrested, Maria Antonia persuaded a stranger heading to San Antonio, Texas to take them on as passengers. Not only did he agree to accept her fifty-dollar offer, but he loaded the old baúl onto his truck. Maria Antonia had at last rescued her father's cherished keepsake.

After their marriage, Maria Antonia and her husband Manuel Castañeda lived in Muzquiz, when she became the stepmother to his two children and they had two of their own during the Muzquiz years. Her two oldest children, Paco and Minerva were born there. Because Manuel Castañeda was an accountant with a mining company owned by the United States, job security kept them from thinking about leaving.

Despite newspapers and radio stations proclaiming "la revolución" had finally ended, it did not end in 1920. Pancho Villa's cavalry, made up of many Yaqui Indians called "Los Dorados," fought in Saltillo, and in Juarez in 1911, but battles and skirmishes raged on well beyond 1920.

Dictator Porfirio Diaz ruled Mexico for more than three decades. When he resigned and went into exile in France, Madero was proclaimed a hero and elected president in 1911. Unfortunately, his victory was short lived. In 1913, Madero was assassinated. What followed were more assassinations and turmoil. Madero's assassination by General Victoriano Huerta stirred vengeance among the warring factions and political organisms. There were Villistas, Zapatistas, Carrancistas and other groups vying for power in Mexico now. Pancho Villa, Emiliano Zapata, and supporters of Carranza held court. Thousands upon thousands of Mexicans had been tortured and executed during the revolution. The civilian population yearned for food and medical supplies, while an entire nation was in ruins. Moreover, despite this distressing backdrop Mexicans held on to hope for a better Mexico than the one they had known under Diaz.

After her marriage, Maria Antonia stayed in touch with her father and her aunts because she lived in Muzquiz, Coahuila. She never wanted to leave her hometown. But one day the mining company closed. Manuel Castañeda and many others had to find work elsewhere. While myriad Mexicans entered the United States, fearing not only unemployment but more bloodshed, she and her husband moved to Laredo. His new job in the border town dissuaded them from leaving Mexico, at first. She had often said that Manuel Castañeda had brains but had no ambition. She worried that his laziness would lead to his dismissal as the town's accountant.

That was the reason Maria Antonia decided to open a café. Despite the challenge of rearing her children and stepchildren, her café flourished. One day, her uncle, Francisco Menchaca, appeared at the door. He was a tall, handsome man who towered among most residents. Having consulted her aunts as to her new address in Laredo, he had journeyed there on horseback to tell Maria Antonia her father had died. Even as she languished in longevity, Maria Antonia remembered that the news of her father's death had devastated her. His death at forty-eight filled her with guilt about having moved so far away from Muzquiz. Realistically, women of that era had no choice but to follow their husbands anywhere. Maria Antonia said,

I took my children and went to Muzquiz immediately. His brothers had made funeral arrangements. As he lay in a wooden casket, the years we had spent together came rolling back. That was the last time I saw my aunts. I was so distraught I didn't even ask about the farm or his belongings. I simply cried until my chest ached from so much grief.

Since her room at the nursing home was too small to hold any of the gifts Maria Antonia had received, Hilda and Anita took the gifts away for safekeeping. They had also put all the greeting cards she had received in a huge manilla envelope. A few days after the celebration, the nursing home director said Maria Antonia could leave the facility for a daylong visit to the home of her closest relative. Jeorge's home was nearby. There she would hear about the wonderful response to her birthday and comments about her return.

After abuelita was helped into Hilda's roomy sport utility vehicle, with Anita in the passenger seat, Maria Antonia realized she was only five minutes from the home of her son, Jeorge, for the first time since her transfer to the Michigan nursing home. Once inside the home Anita announced that she would have to return to Texas the following day. So, she and Hilda thought it was time their abuelita took a close look at the mountain of gifts and opened her greeting cards.

Gloria, Jeorge's wife of over fifty years, sat on the living room couch in anticipation of Maria Antonia's reaction. Anita held up a sleeping gown and suggested she try it on. But Maria Antonia said it was too much trouble. Then she showed her a pair of slippers, which Maria Antonia agreed to slip on, more as a gesture of cooperation than interest in the slippers. She told them, in Spanish,

> I'm sure that all these beautiful nightgowns will fit me just fine. I'm just an old lady who does not go out anymore, so the gowns will be fine. As for the slippers, my feet are always cold, so I know I will use them.

Abuela told her granddaughters, "At my birthday party I noticed there were several envelopes on the table where my birthday cake was. You brought them here along with all the gifts?"

Anita responded, "Sí abuelita, we have them right here."

"Muy bien. ¡Ábrelos todos! Very well, open all of them!"

One by one, Hilda carefully opened each birthday card. As soon as it was opened, either dollar bills or a check flew out. She and Anita gleefully exclaimed this one had cash or that one was a check.

Maria Antonia sat in her borrowed wheelchair simply bobbing her head displaying a half-smile that left the two cousins wondering if she understood her good fortune. When Hilda was finished with every single envelope, reinserting the gift of money, Maria Antonia spoke up. "Just one minute! Now that you've told me the name of the person who wrote me a check or the person who gave me cash for my birthday you need to do something else," Maria Antonia said to the surprise of both granddaughters. "Put the checks in one pile and all the cash in another pile. Then add up each one and give me the total. Soy vieja, pero no pendeja. I may be old but I'm not a fool." The quip made Gloria burst out laughing so hard she fell from the couch on which she had been but a mildly interested spectator.

This incident was told and retold to every member of the family, friends, and nursing home staff, thus eradicating any doubt as to Maria Antonia's sound mind. To Anita, however, this was not the first time her grandmother had risen to the challenge concerning her extraordinary mental alertness. Even at one hundred and three, Maria Antonia kept scrupulous track of her secondary savings account. She did the same with her property taxes, always making sure they were paid. All the utilities, which were in her name only, were paid on time.

By contrast, Minerva was so absent minded she often misplaced her purse, her keys, and even money. She also depended on her mother for money when she spent her own social security check. She often depleted her monthly income buying non-essentials. She was a squanderer who didn't believe in budgets. Maria Antonia often gave her daughter a handful of dollar bills so she could buy groceries. Much as a child reacts when given an unexpected reward, Minerva happily took the money and went shopping.

Predictably, Minerva would return with bags of rose bushes and vitamins, proclaiming what great bargains she had found. But

Maria Antonia would exclaim in Spanish: "Válgame Dios, Minerva! ¡No podemos comer rosas y vitaminas! God Save Us! Rose bushes and vitamins will not satisfy our hunger for food!"

Luckily, there was always more money reserved in case Minerva failed her. Maria Antonia's money-management skills were legendary. That cunning skill played a crucial role in avoiding a nursing home, before her daughter abandoned her.

Each time a representative from a county or state agency knocked on her door, Maria Antonia would lecture the visitor about her independence. She rejected any sort of financial or spiritual help. She often spoke about hard times and how she had proudly declined welfare. She was so proud of what she had been able to achieve, Maria Antonia would chirp about her lifetime in Michigan, never confused about the times she lived there. Sometimes she referenced her first house as "la casa chiquita." It was the first Michigan home when her sons went off to war. "Minerva already had two daughters, your older sisters. But her ex-husband Manuel López moved to New Mexico and never provided child support."

"Then, when your mother returned from months in Mexico, she had you. We needed help with food and other things but accepting welfare meant tolerating home inspections by welfare workers, so we said, 'No.'" Maria Antonia proudly exclaimed.

With toddlers, Mercedes and Martha, and newborn Anita, Maria Antonia had no choice but to become a full-time babysitter, while her daughter worked at a Catholic school. The cafeteria needed people to help prepare meals for dozens of children who attended the largest school in Saginaw.

Meanwhile, Maria Antonia also relied on her youngest son, Beto. Although only seventeen years old, he behaved maturely enough to drop out and take a job to help the family. Beto did not enlist. He went to work on a General Motors assembly factory line in Saginaw. Her son, Jeorge also sent her money. Their combined incomes helped the family survive. Paco served as a paratrooper, but he refused to answer Maria Antonia's letters. He visited his brothers in Saginaw. But each visit erupted into an argument because he confronted Maria Antonia about being arrested by the

U.S. Immigration and Naturalization Services in his teenage years. He blamed his mother for having assumed a fictitious surname after that immigration incident. Maria Antonia didn't respond to his accusations. She quickly left the kitchen table when she sensed his rage. She cried over having inadvertently put her son in a situation that resulted in his arrest. But her tears and request for forgiveness over having used poor judgment were rejected.

There were times, Maria Antonia would remind her son, Paco, that she had to think of her other children. She pleaded with him to understand that she never intended to leave him. She had to return to Dallas to ensure her three youngest children didn't starve.

Perhaps because she had survived Mexico's bloodiest episodes during the Mexican Revolution. Or because her husband had abandoned her, leaving her to fend for herself with four children in tow. Whatever the reason! Abuela remained cautious about finances throughout most of her life.

Maria Antonia never felt financially safe and secure without cash. So early on she had resolved to do whatever it took to have money to feed her children. Another promise she had made to herself as a young, abandoned mother was that she would never bring another man into her home.

"I didn't believe a stepfather could love the children of another man. I could not stand by and see my children spanked or reprimanded by a man who was not their biological father. I was firm in my resolve. I would raise my children alone though I knew it would not be easy. I rejected the mentality that said I needed to find another man."

Maria Antonia would ask Anita, "If a man is not a hard-working individual who makes a commitment to support you and your children, provide food, shelter and health care when needed, then what is the point of your union?"

Not referencing Minerva, abuelita said some women use the excuse of loneliness to settle for any man. Women who had more opportunities than she ever had put themselves and their children at risk by allowing men who merely became bedfellows to avoid the most honorable commitment of marriage. Maria Antonia would relate her own life experience to teach Anita that a strong woman deals with life's challenges without relying on a man. She stressed that if a woman has a child, she should be especially aware that a boyfriend or stepfather may damage the bond between mother and child. During one of many of her lengthy storytelling sessions, Maria Antonia said,

> I could've given my children a stepfather. I was young and even a little pretty. At work, some men used to wink at me. I worked as a seamstress in the Dallas Jewish district. But regardless of how many men flirted with me, I refused to cave into carnal desires. Self-respect was my guide.

Her determination to not enter a "common-law marriage" or another matrimony, whether civil or church-sanctioned, put her at odds with her daughter. But this was not the only point on which daughter and mother disagreed. Although Maria Antonia didn't want to plant the seeds of discord among her only daughters' children and herself, she couldn't help but comment occasionally on how totally irresponsible Minerva had been throughout her life.

Shaking her head left and right, Maria Antonia explained that Manuel was a good man, telling Anita,

> Your mother married Manuel López first. But he had to go fight in World War II. When he returned, he had to get acquainted with his first child, Mercedes who was born while he was in Germany. Shortly after his return, the couple had Martha. Why she left him I will never know.

Then, stroking Anita's auburn colored hair, she added,

> As soon as her divorce was final, Minerva decided to visit her father Manuel in Mexico. The family had stayed in

touch with him through a relative, so this made it easy for Minerva to have a place in Muzquiz. While there, she went to a dance in a nearby town where she met Jesús, and that's how you came about.

Unlike her mother, Minerva had a ravenous desire for what she interpreted as love. Supposedly, Jesús Sosa was love at first sight. She had left her two daughters in Maria Antonia's care, while she spent three months in Mexico.

One night, at the urging of her half-brother Juan, Minerva attended a neighborhood dance. When Jesús asked her to dance a bolero, she knew instantly he was the only man she would ever love. Throughout her life Minerva would tell her daughters that Jesús Sosa was the love of her life.

A divorced woman with two young daughters, for Minerva it was acceptable to live with a man in a common-law marriage. Nobody knew what happened between her and Jesús Sosa, but when she returned from Mexico, she was six weeks pregnant. Maria Antonia received her with open arms at "la casa chiquita." Maria Antonia's wages at a local pickle factory had allowed her to pay cash for the property.

When Minerva returned from Mexico, she hadn't seen four-year-old Mercedes and two-year-old Martha in several weeks, and scarcely showed signs of affection. Beyond a pat on their little heads, she didn't shower her children with hugs and kisses.

Martha had deep black eyes and coal-black hair. She also had darker skin than her older sister. Instead of accepting this fact about the genes involved, Minerva lamented that her second oldest reflected more Mexican Indian traits than Spanish features.

On her final day in Mexico, Minerva left Jesús Sosa a letter while he was at work. Had it not been for the letter, Jesús would've never known she was pregnant. This revelation set in motion his desperate desire to cross the border. He wanted to marry Minerva and be present for the birth of his first child.

Back in Michigan, Minerva told Maria Antonia she had learned to fear the man she loved. She said he would work all week to prove his love and commitment. But on the weekends, he would get drunk and threaten her with a gun. In the end, she realized he was not the man she thought he was. So, she left him.

Minerva did not reveal the letter where she told Jesús about being six weeks pregnant. So, when he appeared at abuelita's doorstep asking for her daughter, Maria Antonia was shocked. Having heard about his violent temper, she slammed the door. Maria Antonia was determined to protect her from a man who dared cross the U.S. border without the proper documents. Despite accusations about Jesús Sosa's violent character, Minerva persuaded her mother to let him enter. Reluctantly, Maria Antonia opened the door and invited a man measuring more than six feet tall to enter. Then she assigned him one of the four metal kitchen chairs tucked under a long gray table. In a demanding tone, Maria Antonia said to Jesús, "Minerva is my only daughter. She is the mother of two girls from a previous marriage. Now you're expecting a child with her. Are you prepared to take on the responsibility of all three children?"

Blessed with a serious face, Jesús Sosa sat and listened to Maria Antonia. His rosy cherub face contrasted with his strapping body lodged in the chair. His shiny green eyes blinked occasionally. Armed with the desire to show that he had repented, Jesús spoke to Maria Antonia in his humblest tone.

> Permit me to say that I do love Minerva. I crossed the border to be with her and with my soon-to-be-born child. I came without proper documentation, so I'm here despite the risk of being deported. I would not do this were it not for the love I feel for Minerva and my unborn child.

Shortly after, the couple traveled to Montana where he had heard there was plenty of work. Minerva's two oldest daughters were once again left in the care of Maria Antonia, with an "I'll send for them later." However, the job didn't pan out and four months later the couple returned to the small town of Alma, Michigan, where Jesús Sosa found work at the local foundry.

Just when Maria Antonia thought that her daughter was finally on the right track, Minerva returned to Saginaw. She was now eight months pregnant and unwilling to remain in common-law-marriage with Jesús Sosa. Again, Maria Antonia received her only daughter with open arms. While apart, Jesús Sosa wrote many letters asking Minerva for forgiveness and informed her that he was living in Saginaw with friends who had helped him find work. Jesús promised he would be a better husband and father, but she didn't answer him.

Unfortunately, one day while he was at work officials from the Department of Immigration and Naturalization Services arrested him. Before his transfer to Eagle Pass, Texas, Jesús spent several weeks in a Saginaw jail. Minerva never visited the love of her life!

From Texas he was deported and returned to Coahuila, Mexico. Minerva made no effort to inform the authorities that she was carrying his child. Jesús Sosa's friends had warned her that he might be deported, but she did nothing. In addition to Minerva's struggles, Maria Antonia recalled tough times when she and her youngest son worked full-time. Without child support from Manuel Lopez for his daughters, and with her daughter pregnant from a deported Mexican national, her daily prayer was to keep working to support the whole family. One day, Maria Antonia nearly swallowed her pride and applied for welfare. Coincidentally, that same day she found more work. Anita was born shortly after at a free clinic run by the Sisters of Charity. These nuns worked in conjunction with St. Joseph's Catholic Church in Saginaw.

Convinced the United States Department of Immigration and Naturalization Services would snatch her granddaughter and deport her, Maria Antonia intervened. While Minerva was sedated following the birth, abuelita told authorities that Anita was Manuel López's daughter.

A relative who had visited Michigan and returned to Mexico also knew Jesús Sosa. After he was deported, a family member had helped Jesús find a job. This same relative had delivered the news that Minerva had given birth to a fair-skinned little girl with green eyes and auburn hair. Upon hearing the joyous news, Jesús even decided to take the risk of deportation a second time. Nothing would keep him from seeing his daughter. In 1954 and five years of saving enough money to help him survive after crossing the Rio Grande and heading north, Jesús returned to Saginaw.

When he came calling again, Minerva was living with her three daughters, her mother, and her brother Beto in "la casa chiquita." This time Maria Antonia greeted him with a huge pail of cold water. Abuelita wanted to let him know he was not welcome. She said, waving her arms while screaming at Jesús Sosa. "What are you doing here? Haven't you done enough? She left you because you drink and threatened to beat her. She's working now and doing fine without you. You can't stay here!"

He looked sheepishly beyond the doorway and saw Anita playing. His eyes welled up with tears as he told Maria Antonia that he had come all this way to see his daughter. Reluctantly, but moved by his apparent sincerity, Maria Antonia allowed him to come inside the house. Then, he told her,

> Minerva had no real reason to leave me. I had found a good job at a factory in the town of Alma. She complained that I was gone all day, and she was lonely. Yes, it's true that I drank on the weekends. But I was happy to stay home with her. She was not happy to stay home. She wanted to go dancing. Take weekend trips.

Maria Antonia, in the most earnest Spanish she could muster, said to him,

> My daughter does not seem to know what she wants out of life. She brought two daughters into the world but divorced their father. Then she struck up a relationship with you that resulted in this beautiful child. The only thing I want is for my daughter to make a good life with one man to raise her children.

When Minerva arrived from her job at a local bakery, she found Jesús Sosa waiting for her with their child. Coy at first, Minerva eventually agreed to go out with him, to talk about their future.

Maria Antonia gave her hand to Anita, as Jesús led her daughter out the door through a screened porch attached to the wood-frame house. Maria Antonia saw "la casa chiquita" as a blessed haven for the whole family in the best and in the worst of times.

Since their birth, Maria Antonia showed great love for her granddaughters. She talked to them in Spanish and used nicknames reflecting her abiding love and dedication to ensure they were happy. She had given Mercedes, the oldest of the three, the nickname "Nenita," while she called Martha "Martita," and Ana, her third granddaughter, became sweet little "Anita."

Minerva and Jesús Sosa resolved their differences and returned to Alma. This time Mercedes and Martha went with Minerva. In their first home in that small farming town, they did well for a few months. It was during that time that immigration raids resulted in the arrest and deportation of Anita's father through Operation Wetback. The community learned that hundreds of thousands of Mexicans workers without documents were deported, along with thousands of American citizens.

Jesús disappeared without a trace from Anita's life. When she was twelve years old, she learned that her father lived in Mexico, and her surname was not that of her half-sisters, Mercedes and Martha López. She often dreamed about searching for her father and thought that knowing his name and that of the Mexican town in Coahuila, where he was born, would be sufficient to find him. To learn about her father, Anita had to rely on bits and pieces of information from the family. There was not a single photograph of him.

Meanwhile, Minerva had gone on with her life and had three more children, totaling five girls and one boy. It wasn't too long before Minerva began complaining about her third husband, Ricardo Peña. She resented him for not officially marrying her until their third child was born. She also complained that he was a miser who habitually locked up cookies, bananas, and other select foods in a kitchen cabinet—he gave access only to his three biological children.

Minerva Castañeda Peña had realized that Ricardo Peña had tricked her into believing he loved her. After articulating these thoughts to her three oldest children, Minerva launched into an extramarital affair with a man several years younger—the affair was short lived because he was deported. Like an unanswered prayer to her obsessive need for freedom, Minerva's third husband died in a tragic car accident. Instead of Minerva, Anita would be the one who felt guilt over his death. That week before his untimely death, Anita had shouted at Ricardo Peña when he told her to put down the bottle of milk because it was not for her.

"I hate you! I hate you. I wish you were dead."

After the outburst, Anita ran out the front door. His miserly ways were more than the child could bear. Her response to him became the first and only time Anita ever disrespected him.

The food incident was followed by a dream Anita had in which Ricardo Peña's cold, lifeless body was laid out in a casket in the middle of their living room. A week later, while she was in the kitchen doing dishes during Easter vacation, Anita heard a knock at the door. The knock at the door stirred in her the feeling that her stepfather was dead. As she ran to open the front door, Anita came face-to-face with the local funeral director at their doorstep. When he asked to speak to her mother, Anita's eyes welled up, as she ran upstairs to get her.

Anita López couldn't stop thinking about what she had told her stepfather days earlier. For the rest of her life, she would feel profound remorse for having allowed words of hate to cross her lips, for she never hated her stepfather. Minerva Castañeda Peña didn't cry over the untimely death of her third husband. None of her children witnessed any emotions or tears at her loss. Instead, Minerva used the church as punishment for Anita, requiring her to go to mass daily.

Anita understood Ricardo Peña had deprived her of milk, but Minerva didn't think her daughter's angry words were justified. That's why she made the child feel she was being punished for her stepfather's death. Her mother told her "Only prayers and going to church could forgive your sin." The reality was that now Minerva Castañeda Peña was free to dabble deeper into free love, a lifestyle she seemed to desire and crave. Shortly after Ricardo Peña's death, Minerva sold their household belongings and took five of her six children on a one-way road trip to California. Seventeen-year-old Mercedes was the only one who escaped the whirlwind trip to San José. She worked in a grocery store after school. The widowed store owner had grown fond of Mercedes, and she had made the family proud, earning a merit-based scholarship to Michigan State University. So, when the owner asked if she could stay on, her mother agreed.

Minerva Castañeda Peña was no barfly. She did not engage in any sort of illicit behavior or drug consumption. She never showed a weakness for alcohol or tobacco. The only human weakness she displayed was the consummate need for a man's attention. From the time she became a widow to the end of her long life, the self-actualized intellectual had her ways to attract men. Within days of arriving in California she had a new man at her side—whom she promptly introduced to her children as a friend—she dated him for the next three months. It only took three months for Minerva to realize she had made a mistake, when a realtor told her to go back to Michigan because it was a better place for her girls, who would otherwise end up in trouble and pregnant. Before long she was behind the wheel of the 1959 Buick heading back to Michigan. Anita and Martha cried as they gazed out at the Camino Real highway, which took them away. Their mother paid them no mind and kept on driving toward Route 66, back to Michigan.

At the urging of Maria Antonia, Minerva did not sell the German-built house her late husband left her. This made it possible for her to return to live with her children in their old neighborhood. Led by Maria Antonia, family members welcomed her back and offered to contribute gently used furniture. The three oldest daughters thought it strange that their mother was able to unlock the front door of the empty house and resume residency so easily.

Anita recalled the day their mother had sold the contents of the entire house, but this was not by chance or a stroke of luck. To the dismay of Mercedes, Martha, and Anita, Minerva Castañeda Peña had stayed in touch by telephone with her previous lover, William Ford. Their courtship began when Mr. Ford extolled the virtues of living as close to the earth as humanly possible. A blue-eyed blond with crooked teeth and bad breath, he proudly declared himself a naturalist. Mr. Ford loved stating that he had been born one hundred years too late. Soon thereafter, Minerva Castañeda Peña sold the Saginaw home and moved north. Three years later, the man she called "Mr. Ford" despite their intimacy suggested she move farther north to an area the family described as "the wilderness" for its thick, untamed wooded area, and total solitude.

This time, it wasn't only Mercedes who refused to go, but also Martha, who would move into the home Maria Antonia shared with her son Jeorge and his family in Saginaw, while Anita's world of living in the city and attending an affordable Catholic school came crashing down. She was a fifteen-year-old teenager when she was plucked from a lifetime of city living and thrown into a life she had never known. And it was not just living in the wilderness that sent her into a deep depression. It was her mother's willingness to live a lifestyle Mr. Ford said was best for her and her children.

Well water was acceptable, but there was no inside bathroom in the house he had built. That was outrageous for Anita. Her mother behaved as if she wasn't in charge of her own life. She was all too willing to bow to his every suggestion, including heating the home with the plentiful chopped wood found on the land she bought. Mr. Ford, a man she kept as her common-law husband for eight years, also denounced city services. He insisted that well water was the best water around. All, including the younger children, were expected to carry water into the house from the well. But they suffered horribly during Michigan winters when they had to trudge through piles of snow and ice to get to the outhouse. Anita was so depressed in the wilderness that she cried as she wrote poem after poem about her loss of friends and family. Her beloved grandmother, cousins, uncles, and aunts were all now an hour away. To a teenager without a car, the distance may as well have been across the country.

As luck would have it, Mercedes bought a used Mercury she drove while attending college. However, she soon realized that the upkeep was not worth the trouble. At Michigan State University, she rode a bicycle to class. After Anita passed a driver's education class, knowing her predicament, Mercedes gave Anita the Mercury. Meanwhile, Martha López had graduated from high school, while living with Maria Antonia. Always in a big hurry to grow up and be on her own, Martha traveled to Dallas on a Greyhound bus to search for her long, lost father, Manuel López.

Determined, Martha persuaded two classmates who had graduated with her to make the move to Dallas. She knew her mother had met her father there in 1941. Her mother even shared that a tree in the city's landmark, Reverchon Park, had their initials engraved in it. Without an idea where to begin the search, Martha went to the Dallas Police Department. Since he had no criminal record, they referred her to another López family who said he had moved to New Mexico. They said he was a chef, a profession he had learned in the U.S. Army, during World War II. Martha López told her sisters what she found.

> When our dad was in the Army, he was assigned kitchen duty. That's where he learned all about being a chef. He took that up as a career when he came back from the war. He worked at the Baker and other luxury hotels in Dallas before moving away.

With that information, Martha took a Greyhound bus to meet him in New Mexico. During the two weeks she stayed, they bonded. While she was still there visiting, he called Minerva Castañeda Peña to say he wanted to see his oldest daughter. Anita never forgot the call and would recall how it changed her life.

She also recognized the many ways she hated Mr. Ford's dominance and unorthodox ideas. So, she jumped at the chance to join her sister.

When she heard, Mercedes was going to meet her biological father, Anita begged her to ask him if she could go along as her first ever summer vacation. Manuel agreed, after obtaining permission from their mother. To make her journey feasible, Mercedes told Anita to raise $50 dollars to buy her own roundtrip airline ticket. Anita took note about how unhappy she had been and came up with a solution. She sold the Mercury for $50 and bought a round-trip ticket on a plane bound to New Mexico from Michigan. Now sixteen years old, Anita had resolved to escape Mr. Ford's dominance, at least for a while.

Neither of the young sisters had ever been on an airplane. The mandatory stopover in Chicago's O'Hare Airport was mindboggling. This was 1966 and it looked as if there were more soldiers and sailors in the airport than civilians. Unbeknownst to the sisters, this was at the peak of the Vietnam war.

An unexpected flight delay meant the sisters would have to spend the night sprawled out on the airport floor or chairs. Once they settled into a comfortable position, Anita noticed many military personnel had done the same. Intent on getting to their destination, the following day they ran toward their assigned gate.

The tearful encounter between Manuel López and Mercedes brought tears to Anita's own eyes. From that moment on, Anita deepened her desire to search for her father in Mexico. Still, she had no clue where to begin or how she would do it. In the meantime, she was grateful her sister's father had taken her in. Manuel López was a soft-spoken man with a gentle spirit. During the two weeks the girls stayed with him and his wife, he embraced his teenage stepdaughter, Anita, as if she were his own.

When they were ready to go home, Manuel López offered to take the girls with him, since he was traveling to Dallas to visit his sister, and the flight from Dallas to Michigan would be much easier. To their surprise, they learned that Martha had moved to Dallas with two classmates. The eighteen-year-old girls were recent high school graduates. They were eager to begin their lives in a new state. Because of the stories Maria Antonia had told her about the jobs she had held while living there, Martha López was inspired to visit Dallas for the first time. This was especially the case, when she learned that her mother and uncles had attended several schools in Dallas—the most fashionable Texas city.

Among the many things she learned from abuelita was the difficulties they experienced during the Great Depression. Martha was most impressed to know that schoolteachers thought Minerva and her brothers didn't need charity because they were well dressed. Maria Antonia spent all her money on her four children. An excellent seamstress, what she couldn't buy she made. Her description of Dallas, close friends, businesses and customs filled Martha with the necessary courage to travel to this big city in search of her father. The Dallas Police Department was also able to locate her twice-married aunt, Laura López, who made the connection to Manuel López.

Minerva had a great deal of help from Maria Antonia raising her children in Michigan. Nevertheless, when Martha exhausted her patience, Minerva would tell her that she had taken after her aunt Laura López. It wasn't a compliment, but a disparaging observation. If that were not enough, Minerva Castañeda Peña's references to her daughter's cinnamon-colored skin, also had a negative impact. Maria Antonia's acceptance of the derogatory comments, nicknaming her "India macuasa," and stories about her unmarried, bar-hopping aunt contributed to Martha's rebellious nature. Even though, Maria Antonia tried to assure Martha that she was loved, and there was a time Anita thought she was Maria Antonia's favorite granddaughter, Martha was severely damaged by her environment. When they reunited in Dallas, Anita realized how deeply scarred her half-sister had been by their mother's put downs growing up.

Nobody ever knew for sure, but speculation among family members galvanized the conclusion that being called "India macuasa" as a child resulted in Martha's self-destructive behavior. Minerva never said where she found that nickname for her second daughter. But anytime she was angry about something she suspected Martha had done she would holler "India macuasa you did it!" And when those two words emerged from her lips in anger, and landed on Martha's pre-adolescent frame, it made her feel worthless. In her tragic teen years, Martha recalled being saddled with a nickname worse than those given to Mercedes and Anita. Mercedes known as "flaca," meaning skinny in Spanish, or "galga," which is a female greyhound dog in Spanish. Anita was "la güera" because of her fair skin and hazel eyes.

Once Martha grew up and went out on her own in Dallas, she seemed to accept her dark, Asian looks together with the derogatory nickname. She may even have surmised that she was born to be bad. She took to declaring proudly to friends, family and casual acquaintances, that she was the black sheep of the family. Turning the stigma into a protective shield to hide the hurt of being rejected by her mother, Martha began to spiral downward, so that in 1967 she began smoking marijuana. Since she had taken up smoking in her senior year, she didn't regard the strange smell of the cigarette as harmful. Minerva would say smoking pot was a step up from regular smoking and that her grandmother had spoiled her to the point that Martha didn't fear the consequences to her health or the harm to her future.

Minerva said that worse yet was the fact that Martha seemed to challenge any authority, including the law. Minerva never once blamed herself for any of her daughter's bad behavior. She was quick to blame her mother, and she never tired of saying Martha had inherited her aunt's bad genes. Minerva would lament, not willing to acknowledge that her example was not in line with what they were learning in school, often saying, "I sent my three oldest daughters to a Catholic school so the sisters could educate them and teach them religious behavior, but it was a waste of time with Martha. She always takes the wrong road!"

Maria Antonia continued to show Martha López love regardless of what her daughter said. She would always talk to Martha about her dreams and aspirations in the most loving way. Just as she did with Anita, Maria Antonia reminded Martha that she had tended to her and rocked her to sleep as a baby, cooing to her. "Mi alma, cariño. ¿Dile a tú abuelita que te pasa? My soul, mi love, tell your granny what's wrong." Even though she would not share the secrets in Martha's tortured soul, Maria Antonia's choice of loving words elevated her granddaughter's spirit.

Many-a-time, abuela told Martha to confide in her. "Tell me what's troubling you." Then, abuela would lovingly say to her, and all her granddaughters, that they filled her life with happiness. Maria Antonia enjoyed reminding them how she had cradled them as infants and changed their diapers as babies. She would often tell her three oldest granddaughters, who understood Spanish,

The love of a grandmother is eternal. The love I feel for my grandchildren is more than I ever imagined. I love the other children Minerva had with Ricardo Peña. But you

139

three girls are more like my own daughters. I helped raise you since birth.

If Minerva Castañeda Peña ever heard Maria Antonia say this in her presence, she would become enraged. Minerva would attack her mother verbally. She would accuse Maria Antonia of kidnapping Mercedes and Martha López when they were only toddlers, ignoring the fact that she had left them and gone to live with Jesús Sosa. In the most accusatory manner, Minerva Castañeda Peña screamed,

> You took the girls without my permission! When I returned to Saginaw from Montana with Jesús and my baby, Anita, you had left for Traverse City. You knew I was coming back. You didn't need to take them with you, so the law would say you kidnapped them.

WHENEVER MINERVA created chaos, Maria Antonia sat quietly waiting for her daughter to calm down. In the case of taking the girls, abuelita would explain that she didn't know where she had gone with Jesús Sosa, or if she would be back. Maria Antonia defended her decision, never denying she had taken the girls. But, in-between Minerva Castañeda Peña's frenzied screaming accusations, Maria Antonia said she feared Minerva would leave the girls with strangers.

In these quarrels, Anita and her older sisters never took sides. Instead, Minerva's eldest girls gave their mother the benefit of the doubt. Between their mother and her self-sacrificing mother, they grew up hearing continuous discord. Yet, they noted early on that Minerva never acknowledged her mother's help.

Still, when mother and daughter were on good terms—a rare event—they often burst out laughing. If the girls heard them, they would look at one another in amazement. Unfortunately, those joyous moments between Maria Antonia and Minerva were short-lived.

Surprisingly, Michigan's Mexican Civic Union became the bridge that led to a truce. The social group needed a dance instructor. Even though she lacked a formal dance education, Minerva volunteered. Since her daughters had rejected becoming ballerinas, Minerva turned her attention to teaching dance and choreography. Members of the social group were delighted to have someone teach their children ballet, folk dances, and the like for free. She learned the dances that she taught the children to perform on stage—it made their parents proud. In addition, the original routines she had devised were her own choreographic creations.

This social organization was a source of pride to the newly arrived Mexican immigrants who had passports or green cards allowing them to work. Maria Antonia's talent as a seamstress and her willingness to help, proved to be a rousing success in the German/Polish dominated Saginaw of the 1950s. At last, Minerva had found her calling.

Among their performances there was a memorable stage scene requiring Anita to play the bull, while Martha played matador. The routine was created to "The March of the Toreadors" from Bizet's opera, *Carmen*. Mainly composed of parents whose children were in the program the audience loved the unique musical. In the 1950s, when mambo was all the rage, Minerva chose her daughter Martha to star in a mambo-themed program in which her costume was made of a dozen colorful balloons. However, when balloons began popping, the poor child rushed off the stage in a flood of tears. To everyone's surprise, they gave her a standing ovation as they chanted "Martha. Martha. Martha." They coaxed her back onto the stage. Amid thunderous applause, Martha reappeared in a gold, glittery two-piece costume capable of withstanding the rigorous movement of her shoulders during a lively performance.

While Minerva lived her dream of dancing and choreography, her three youngest children were being tended to by her docile husband. Since he loved cooking, he did that as well. Like most Mexican immigrants, Ricardo Peña was a blue-collar worker at General Motors. Still, he helped his wife at home. As long as Maria Antonia was willing to remain hunched over her Singer sewing machine creating costumes for hours on end, Minerva kept dreaming up more skits and stage scenes. She had routines for Easter, Christmas, Thanksgiving Day, and the Fourth of July. Minerva's ideas were limitless, as was her energy.

After a couple of years, her husband and the stepfather to three of her oldest daughters, told her she had to get a real job—one that paid. Reluctantly, Minerva gave up her dancing ambitions and found employment in a bakery. When she ballooned to nearly 200 pounds, Minerva's working days were over.

A self-taught individual who yearned for a better life even as a child, Minerva used to tell Anita and her sisters about the hate she had for picking cotton in Texas. She said Maria Antonia scolded her and made her work alongside her, while praising her three brothers. In the fields, Minerva stubbornly resisted and daydreamed about growing up and becoming an important person. She felt all the riches she desired were out there for the taking, and while Minerva didn't know exactly how she would rise above her status, she was determined to keep her children from ever doing backbreaking migratory work. She told her girls that the states where Maria Antonia had negotiated a contract to work were Illinois, Ohio, Michigan, and others. Maria Antonia called Minerva and put her in her place telling her they were destined to work in the fields. As she did with her sons, she tried to persuade Minerva to believe hard work defined a person's self-worth. If it was honorable, it didn't matter what kind of work it was. Her daughter rejected her mother's outlook and turned to reading as many books as she could when she wasn't required to work.

By age sixteen, Minerva had read books on American and Spanish history, music, philosophy, religion, and dance. She memorized the lives of great composers such as Beethoven, Mozart, Strauss, and others. She often said that when she heard classical music, the hairs on her arms would stand up. Predictably, the constant obligation to travel to other states to work, coupled with absence from school, led her to drop out before graduating. Maria Antonia didn't question Minerva's decision. All she knew was that she needed her children to work alongside her to earn enough money to survive.

Maria Antonia often told her grandchildren that her boys were hard workers who never gave her any trouble. Then she'd say Minerva, on the other hand, hated agricultural work. Maria Antonia credited backbreaking migratory field work as the reason her three sons had a strong work ethic. Sometimes, she would even suggest her sons had inherited her Spanish Basque toughness and rugged individualism. Minerva, by comparison, had inherited Manuel Castañeda's complacency. Maria Antonia often pleaded with Manuel to go find work or get up and go to work, before he left her. She clarified,

Manuel was a smart man who earned a good salary as the accountant for the mining company, but he had no ambition. Often, he overslept and was late for work, even when I was up before dawn and had his breakfast on the table.

Maria Antonia would argue that genetics were associated with his laziness. She would often make that case for her children, when speaking about Manuel's distaste for work. Maria Antonia would ask them,

Where does laziness come from? It comes from your bloodline. There are many things we as human beings inherit from parents and grandparents. In his case, I'm sure Manuel inherited his attitude from someone in the family. Maybe from a relative he had never met. Regardless of where he got it, Manuel was always too tired to go to work.

It wasn't a surprise to Maria Antonia, when one fine day the mining company laid off Manuel, they no longer needed him. Her oldest was two and her daughter a newborn. That's when Maria Antonia began worrying about feeding the family, which included Manuel Castañeda's two older children. Raised by her aunts in the Catholic faith, Maria Antonia turned to the blessed virgin and several saints for help. She began going to church daily, lighting traditional candles reserved for special requests, begging the blessed mother of Jesus Christ to find her husband a new job. To deal with her situation, Maria Antonia relied on her father's words about her and his ethnic people.

Her father, Roque Menchaca, had told her one distinguishing feature of Basque women was that they were spiritually stronger, and on rare occasions, even physically stronger than men. These women of the earth often adapted to dire situations, even when those were physically challenging. Her father would tell Maria Antonia that she had inherited the traits found in Basque women, recalling his words while feeling anxious about the future.

Now that Manuel was unemployed, she placed him in charge of the children and went to work. She knew that with the help of Manuel's oldest biological daughter, he could handle the responsibilities. Maria Antonia soon found work in a nearby cafe. Her love of cooking coupled with her ability to season food to perfection quickly endeared her to the cafe owner. Sufficiently impressed with her abilities, he asked her to reorganize the menu.

Ten months later, Manuel Castañeda found work in Nuevo Laredo, Mexico. After a neighbor, who had just returned from visiting a relative told him a local company was looking for an accountant, Manuel traveled there to apply. Having withstood the daily challenges of caring for two young children and supervising the older ones, Manuel Castañeda was eager to return to his profession. The family moved to Nuevo Laredo, where he vowed to stop drinking so as not to jeopardize his good paying job.

Maria Antonia's refined aunts had taught her a slew of recipes, but she prided herself most on making traditional desserts. Her delicious capirotada, a traditional bread pudding prepared and enjoyed during Lent, was popular with her new neighbors. Friends and neighbors said Toña's sweet pumpkin and camote-filled empanadas were an authentic gastronomical ecstasy. Grandchildren raved about abuelita's empanadas as well as her buñuelos, torrijas—a type of French toast—and even her homemade apple pie. While cooking at home, one day, Maria Antonia told Anita,

I've owned two restaurants, one in Nuevo Laredo and one in Saginaw. I think people like my cooking because I put love

144

into everything I make. I also try to give my customers an extra little something or what we call pilón on their plate.

Anita recalled that if she ever wanted Mexican food, she had to visit her abuelita. Her mother hated cooking so much that when she tried it, it came out raw or burned. Faced with the daily job of feeding six children, their mother relied on fruits, vegetables, and frozen foods.

Maria Antonia's father told her that some of Mexico's food such as papas con huevo, egg and potatoes, originated in Spanish cuisine. For example, Mexico's popular potato and egg breakfast began as the traditional Spanish tortilla or Spanish omelet. Another dish she prepared was the proverbial Mexican style "menudo" or tasty tripe. This dish, synonymous with Mexico, was usually spicy. In Spain a dish called "Callos a la Madrileña" was similar except it was not as spicy. On Christmas Eve, another Spanish tradition of serving cod fish or bacalao also graces many Mexican tables.

Spain ruled Mexico for 300 years, so its gastronomic influence is clear and undeniable. Maria Antonia's aunts passed the traditions to their young niece who learned how to prepare several dishes. She became so adept at food preparation and appetizing presentation that she was asked to open a restaurant. Maria Antonia would often tell her friends, when they suggested it, "I have a two-year-old boy and a baby girl. Now that Manuel is working, I am unable to es-tablish a restaurant. Besides, I have no extra help because Manuel's older children are in school all day."

Not one content to sit back and wait for the perfect opportu-nity, Maria Antonia began selling her homemade meals to the local colonias or barrios in and around Nuevo Laredo. From scraps of boxes discarded by a paper business nearby, her ingenuity led her to create her own packaging. One day, after several weeks of cooking from the stove in her rented home, Maria Antonia was approached by the city's mayor. He liked her cooking so much he offered her space in an empty building he owned. Toward that end he went to visit her and, introducing himself, told her,

> My name is José Antonio Castellanos, and I am very impressed with your cooking. My wife and children love your enchiladas, which we tasted when we bought your packaged meals. Your good food is why I've come to offer you space so you can open a cafe restaurant.

Over Manuel's objections, she kept her children in an adjoining room while she prepared most of the daily menu. She recruited a server and trained her to arrange the food on a plate so that it looked irresistible, she also assisted in the kitchen when necessary. Maria Antonia told the server, "I can't pay you because I am just starting out, but you will get tips and gain restaurant experience just like I did. With this work you will go far and may even start your own business someday."

The Taco Rico opened for business. Her husband would come home from work and sulk. He didn't like the idea of his wife working again. He said the neighbors would talk about him and accuse him of not being man enough to support his family. As he sank in his armchair with the local newspaper, Maria Antonia would retort: "People who talk will always talk. The best we can do is ignore them. They're jealous of those who have the courage and ambition to work hard to rise above their situations." Maria Antonia reminded Manuel,

> My family, which means my uncles in Muzquiz, have all had their own businesses. I'm just as able and qualified to have my own business. I know I am not formally educated, but I will pay my taxes, and, to make sure they are in order, you can look over my books.

She added, "There are jobs done by men that women can do, if pressed."

Maria Antonia was the most selfless woman Anita had ever known. And it wasn't because she bragged about herself, it was because every once in a rare moment, when Minerva was not berating Maria Antonia, she would tell her children about a kind act her mother had done. By way of an example, she recalled that one time Anita López was visiting two women in San Antonio. Minerva said, "Toña used to take a huge pot of coffee and pan dulce to the prisoners in a chain gang. When she saw them sweating and working on the city streets, Maria Antonia felt sorry for them." Another instance that Minerva shared was when they were children. "Sometimes Toña would give our food away to others. Even though we never lacked food or went hungry, we couldn't understand why Toña always gave away our food."

In the very few stories Minerva told Anita, she never forgot the one about her uncle—it was about Maria Antonia's love and determination to save her son, Jeorge, when he was six years old and had been running a high fever for three days. Aside from vomiting, Jeorge had developed a rash over most of his body and laid in bed nearly lifeless. As was her practice, Maria Antonia relied on home remedies to bring down the fever. Popular in Mexico, she rubbed him with volcanic oil and gave him brewed tea from herbs in her garden. But nothing helped. Not one to seek medical attention, Maria Antonia finally relented and told the children to close the doors and keep them locked, instructing them not answer it to anyone while she went in search of a doctor.

The lack of transportation and the distance did not dissuade her. Maria Antonia scooped her son out of bed and trudged along with him in her arms. She had walked almost a mile when a farmer offered to take them in his pick-up truck. The nearest town was five miles up the road in Dallas. Breathless and exhausted, Maria Antonia looked down on her son's sweaty face and knew she had to accept help. Although fearful of strangers, she lifted Jeorge into the truck and prayed for a miracle. In the end, her son recovered from the unexplained illness at a state-run clinic in the city of Dallas.

Aside from her own immediate family, helping others throughout her life was the reason so many people remember Maria Antonia. A born entrepreneur, she always imagined owning her own business and she loved to earn her own money.

ANITA REMEMBERED those afternoon or late evening visits to abuelita. Often, she found abuela sound asleep. During those waiting periods, when abuela took too long to respond, Anita imagined the worst. She envisioned abuelita had suffered a stroke, a heart attack, or death. Anita can still capture the joy of hitting the second story bedroom windows with several pebbles, which finally woke abuelita.

In a state of drowsiness, abuelita opened the bedroom window shouting, "¿Eres tú, Anita? Me encontraste dormida, pero ya te voy a abrir la puerta, cariño. Is that you, Anita? You found me sleeping, but I'm going to open the door, love." Anita breathed a sigh of relief to know she was okay.

Now, on her visit, upon entering the room, she found her in her assigned bed at the nursing home. Anita lovingly gazed at abuelita, wondering how much longer she would last now that she didn't reside in her cherished San Antonio home.

Many times, when visiting her grandmother, she saw abuela's wrinkled face and cotton-white hair pushing aside the curtains. She also heard about the many hardships she faced throughout the years. Still, what made Anita most proud was those stories about her generosity and empathy with family members and strangers.

Gina Peña Schmidt, Minerva's oldest daughter from her marriage to Ricardo Peña, married the boy next door. A tall, lanky, blue-eyed blonde, Gary Schmidt, had watched Mr. Ford build the house intended for Minerva and her children. Gina's husband was inquisitive as a boy and learned quickly about how to survive with little money or a formal education beyond high school. Mature beyond his eighteen years, Gary had already learned much, from how to build a house to raising chickens and milking cows. Gina and Gary had both attended a nearby country school that offered a marginal public Michigan education. With no money or staff to promote higher education beyond high school, a formal education was out of their reach. However, through his own initiative, Gary became an expert mechanic while Gina worked in a nursing facility.

One day while Gary was changing the oil in a customer's Chevy truck, a tiny bit of oil fell into his eye. A visit to the local doctor revealed he would need emergency surgery. As soon as Maria Antonia heard about Gary's eye, she told Minerva to withdraw $200 dollars from the bank—Minerva obeyed knowing she had no way of paying for an operation. Anita realized the scope of this gesture immediately. She was an elderly woman whose social security benefits amounted to less than $500 a month, and to make ends meet, she rented the two apartments on the first floor of her house for $45 a week. Yet she didn't think twice about using her savings to help save an in-law's eyesight. Maria Antonia was altruistic to the core.

Early in their marriage, Vicente Mas and Anita had benefitted from her compassion. When Vicente received an honorable discharge from the military, the young couple returned to Michigan. As a first-year student, he was accepted to the local community college. Their problem was that they didn't have any savings or credit cards. Their only source of income was going to be the Government Issued GI Bill, which would enable Vicente to attend school and help with financial support. A month before Vicente Mas was scheduled to start, the check failed to arrive. They moved from Missouri, where he had been stationed, to Michigan. What saved them was that the couple had managed to string together a couple of paychecks to pay for a rented truck. During the time Maria Antonia was away, Anita López and Vicente Mas arrived in Michigan, with no place to begin their life anew. When abuelita got wind of the situation, she offered the couple her new home rent-free saying, "I built a casita on Mercedes's land after I left my son, Jeorge. It's a good, solid wooden house with a very deep well, which cost me $800 dollars."

Maria Antonia's generosity came in handy. Once again, with her savings, abuelita found a way to build a tiny home on the five-acre parcel Mercedes had purchased. As a single female executive with a government job, she was doing well, and had no plans for the land, so she agreed to let Maria Antonia build a tiny house on the land where the family could reside rent-free.

On the other hand, Mercedes had invited her sister, Martha, to live with her in the nation's capital, with the hope that she would finally finish her college degree in film and communications. It wasn't until the two sisters began sharing an apartment in the city center, that Mercedes learned Martha, her biological sister, suffered from schizophrenia. They had never been close and they'd often been at odds with each other over one thing or another. Mercedes had not seen Martha since their father's failed attempt to unite with them in Dallas.

One day, Mercedes came to terms that she could not cope with her sister's illness. A desperate phone call prompted abuelita to fly to Washington, D.C. to help with her sister's diagnosed mental condition. There, Martha received a letter from the university letting her know she would receive scholarship money to finish her degree plan. Nonetheless, Martha decided to stay in Dallas, with the intention of attending El Centro College. But once under her father's roof, Martha would not follow his house rules. The curfew her father set seemed incomprehensible to the young rebel. Manuel López had tried for a year to unite his two oldest daughters with his youngest in Dallas. It was to no avail. His children were strangers to him, as they were to one another. So, he returned to his job as a chef for a hotel in New Mexico.

Vicente and Anita thanked her profusely for her generosity. That's when Maria Antonia told Anita that Martha was very ill. On that call abuelita also told her,

> I need to stay here in Washington to take care of Martha. Your sister, Mercedes, has a good job that keeps her away most of the day, so she can't look after her. I am going to try to persuade Martha to go back to Michigan and live with me in my new house. Until that happens, I want you and Vicente to live there.

Since Maria Antonia was not aware of Martha's propensity to dabble in alcohol, drugs, and unorthodox behavior, abuelita was not convinced her precious granddaughter was mentally ill. Abuela believed that Martha's self-destructive behavior was the result of not feeling loved, even though Maria Antonia had favored Martha growing up. This went unnoticed by Anita because her grandmother never showed a preference for one granddaughter over the other. But Anita had heard Minerva say that Martha was her favorite and that she spoiled Martha to her detriment.

Still, Maria Antonia was determined to cure her through profound love. She was sure that once they were together, Martha would reveal her pain and Maria Antonia would be there to comfort and understand her. Abuela often reiterated in Spanish. "Yo las crie desde que nacieron. I raised you from the time you were born," emphasizing her role as a surrogate mother for Mercedes, Martha, and Anita. That was one of the reasons she didn't hesitate to help when she heard Anita was returning to Michigan.

Anita and Vicente had planned to live with Maria Antonia and Anita's younger siblings. She would work full time until he graduated from college. Although he preferred to live with his wife and their fourteen-month-old son elsewhere, Vicente concluded they had no choice but to accept Maria Antonia's offer. The couple was ecstatic to know they had a place to live rent-free until they were settled. Anita was thrilled to have found a job. And he looked forward to receiving the G I Bill. Unfortunately, and to their dismay, the house had no plumbing. What good was a nice deep well without plumbing?

Distraught at the situation, Anita screamed,

What in the world are we going to do? We have a place to sleep but we need water to cook with and bathe. Nobody told us the house had no plumbing. We can't live here; no way can we live here.

Vicente Mas had inherited a gift his wife didn't know about for many years. He learned quickly and installed or repaired home fixtures without any formal training. An organic handyman, which would pay off years later when the couple bought their first home in Texas, Vicente installed plumbing in Maria Antonia's newly built one-bedroom home. Unafraid of the task at hand, Vicente simply bought a soft-cover book at the local hardware store and went to work. Prior to his triumphant plumbing endeavor, Anita had hauled buckets of water from Minerva's home to Maria Antonia's. This was a grueling experience Anita López would never forget, adding to her lifelong feelings of insecurity.

The lack of running water in his first month out of the secure net of military service had the opposite effect on Vicente Mas. He was filled with such pride at having installed plumbing that he approached his full-time college schedule filled with great expectations. He would tell Anita, "If I can learn to be a plumber, I can do anything. I know it is going to be hard for me, since I have not been in school for years, but I know I can finish in four," Vicente proudly told her.

Maria Antonia had developed a cautious acceptance of Vicente Mas since he had married Anita. At first, Maria Antonia worried Anita was too young to marry. Abuela had cautioned her granddaughter about getting married before the time was right, having been a child-bride herself at seventeen. Aware that Anita had to work so Vicente could study, abuela was now more concerned than ever. She feared Vicente would abandon her granddaughter and great-grandson upon graduation from college. Although it sounded as if she was overreacting, Maria Antonia's fears were not entirely unfounded.

During Vicente's four years in college, the couple saw working spouses abandoned by college graduate husbands. In fact, "putting hubby through degree" acquired its own tongue-in-cheek acronym known as the PhD of working wives. Anita López shared Maria Antonia's fears with her husband. Predictably, he was surprised, as well as insulted. He did not like being perceived as a man capable of abandoning his wife and child. In fact, he said he had no respect for any man who would do that, exclaiming "You know me, Anita! You must know I will never leave you after I graduate! I have been studying so hard to make you proud of me. To ensure we have a future together and with our children."

Anita had met Vicente while she lived in Dallas. Like her abuelita, he too was an immigrant. But unlike most immigrants, he had come the United States to visit his sister in Texas, and, on that summer vacation, he fell in love with rock and roll music and hamburgers. Raised in a middle-class family in Colombia, he'd grown up with parents, family love, confidence, and self-esteem. Consequently, he was sure that with love and the financial assistance of his wife he would succeed.

Years later Vicente Mas would share that he felt a huge responsibility to succeed because he was a married college student with a family. He knew that they depended on him, and that he couldn't disappoint them. Another reason he was determined to graduate was to make his parents proud.

Vicente braved the snowstorms in Michigan, and those four years were a sacrifice for someone not raised in cold weather. And even though the couple had bought land cheaply during those years, he was determined to move to a warmer climate upon graduation from college. Anita López thought the land and her desire to settle in her home state would eventually change her husband's mind. But as he approached the end of his university life, Vicente became more vocal about leaving Michigan, as he attempted to convince Anita that his mind was made up about leaving.

> Your idea about moving to your home state to study was a good one. But living here and going to the university has been hard. I had never lived in a place where it snowed so much and the winters were so cold.

Since she had lived in Dallas and met him there, there was no argument about relocating to Texas. During the four years since their arrival in Michigan, Anita and Vicente had lived for graduation day.

Vicente Mas felt that purchasing several acres of virgin wooded land had not been a waste, even if they did not build a house on it as Anita had wanted. They would simply pay annual taxes and keep it as an investment. More complications would come their way, as the couple was unaware Minerva had persuaded abuela to move to Texas, urging her mother to retire after tolerating Michigan winters since the 1940s. At the same time the young couple relocated, mother and daughter moved to San Antonio in 1976.

Maria Antonia's family members, including her two sons and their wives, were shocked to hear mother and daughter had decided to move far away from home. Jeorge and his wife insisted they had never asked Maria Antonia to move out of their new home, recalling,

> On the day she moved out, it was very hot. We had all been out back planting vegetables on half an acre. She kept telling everyone to move faster, move faster, pushing us to work as if we were migrant workers.

Jeorge clarified,

> I bought these ten acres in cash to build a big house for all of us … to have a vegetable garden or fruit trees … my wife and children are not migrant workers. This is now our permanent home, and mother was offended when I asked her to ease up on them.

Minerva told the family that they had decided Texas was a good retirement place. In her view, they had tolerated bitter cold Michigan weather long enough. Now that the house she had bought while Jeorge was at war had been sold, abuela would rely on her share of the money to move to Texas. Abuela also cashed her life insurance policy. For Minerva, since Mr. Ford, the man her children had considered a stepfather for eight years, was no longer in her life, she could justify her decision by saying that all her children were adults, and they could fend for themselves, telling her brother Jeorge and his wife, "Gina is twenty and plans to marry the boy next door. Julián is eighteen and works in a large grocery store. Seventeen-year-old Eva is going with us. Julián will live in my house and take care of it."

The news that Maria Antonia and Minerva were going to live together spread like wildfire. Family members thought there was something strange about them living together. The two had a long history of arguing, bickering, and never demonstrated their love. Moreover, no one in the entire family had ever heard Minerva call Maria Antonia, mother. For Minerva, she was always Toña. Her father, Roque Menchaca, often called her "Toñita," to denote affection.

Around age nine, Anita asked her mother why she didn't call her grandmother mother or mamá. She said it was Maria Antonia's fault because she hadn't insisted when they were children. Yet Anita occasionally heard her sons call Maria Antonia mamá. Over the years, people quit asking why she called her biological mother, Toña. It just became so common that nobody gave it a second thought. Not a single person in the family ever saw mother and daughter embrace. The two never kissed or hugged, even a casual kiss on the cheek on holidays or special events. This became a source of curiosity for Anita López. How could a mother and daughter never embrace? What had caused alienation between mother and daughter? Did this start in her mother's childhood? Anita was a skillful observer of human behavior.

Many other family members had interesting stories to tell anyone who was curious. Although Maria Antonia's stories are the ones that captured Anita's imagination, she also learned about the trials and tribulations of other family members. Not one to reminisce on growing up, Minerva rarely if ever spoke about her own heartbreaking experiences as a child in Dallas schools. So, when she shared some of those poignant memories, it took her daughters by surprise.

Minerva was painfully shy as a child. In fact, she was such a quiet little girl that friends and family alike wondered if she was deaf and dumb. She couldn't say why she was so shy but she did say that her outrageously long hair contributed to her silence and caused her great anxiety in school. She wanted to cut her hair short, but Maria Antonia insisted she keep it long. Before Maria Antonia gave in, her hair had grown way past her buttocks. That was only when the principal of Cumberland Hill public school in Dallas sent Maria Antonia a note in Spanish demanding her daughter get a haircut.

On one occasion when Minerva was willing to talk about her sad upbringing, she recalled she always had to go to the bathroom during class in school. Minerva said that Maria Antonia gave her a cup of coffee each morning for breakfast, and it invariably triggered the need to go to the bathroom. This became another source of shame in a child who was already painfully shy. She recounted that sometimes a teacher would ignore her hand waving in the air to ask permission to go to the bathroom. This prompted her to jump from her desk and head down the hall before she had a humiliating accident. Minerva would say,

> Toña was so cruel to give me coffee with my breakfast. I couldn't hold it through any class and I was so ashamed when a teacher wouldn't give me permission to go. She probably thought I wanted to get out of the lesson. But I was trying to keep from peeing in my pants.

Anita and her two oldest sisters didn't know what to think about giving coffee to a child. They wondered if that was normal back in the 1930s. Maybe milk was scarce or not available after coupons were issued to families for food supplies during the Great Depression. Regardless of what their mother told them, Mercedes, Martha, and Anita never questioned their grandmother about the long hair or her reaction to coffee. Minerva grew up to be a lifelong coffee drinker. In fact, she would get headaches without a daily cup of coffee or two.

Rarely did she admit that thanks to her mother, she and her brothers didn't often qualify to receive help in terms of food from a welfare agency or social services. Schoolteachers never suspected the family worked seasonal migratory jobs until habitual absences revealed their true status. Minerva proudly recalled,

> As soon as she got paid, Toña would buy material and make me beautiful new dresses. She made sure we bathed every other day, and she braided my long hair. I went to school so well-dressed and so well-groomed no one knew our mother was the sole provider.

No one ever suspected the family survived by following the migrant stream—they were migrant workers.

Everyone in the entire Castañeda Menchaca family had the privilege of growing up hearing Maria Antonia's wise Spanish idioms. She made sage and colorful comments often, and when she felt the topic of conversation was just right. For example, Minerva would relate with a hearty laugh "She used to say, 'Cuando digo que el gato es pardo, es porque tengo los pelos en la mano.'" The English translation, "If she knew the cat's color it was because she had a fistful of its fur." Maria Antonia could prove whatever she said. Unlike her brothers, Minerva raised her children in the Spanish language by the book before home schooling was in vogue. But while they became adept at translating Spanish idioms, sometimes they did not clearly understand the intended message in Maria Antonia's vernacular, once it was translated to English. When she wasn't making thought-provoking pronouncements in Spanish, Maria Antonia would use riddles and jokes to get a point across. Her daughter didn't like her jokes at all. She thought they were often inappropriate and not funny. Minerva said her mother invented riddles nobody but her could ever answer. For example, "Toña likes to tell a riddle about a girl who was wearing a short skirt while roller skating." 'Well, one day the girl fell.' Then Maria Antonia would follow up with, 'What do you think anyone passing by saw?'" Minerva shook her head upon hearing her mother ask a family member or a friend to answer the riddle. Obviously, anyone would respond that they saw her underwear.

Maria Antonia, on the other hand, would say "this was a harmless riddle that illustrated something about a person's mind. She would explain that what anyone passing by saw that the girl did not yet know how to roller skate." If she had known how to roller skate, she wouldn't have fallen.

Maria Antonia defended her fondness of riddles and jokes, offering that they were discrete ways of communicating or imparting a lesson or a moral message. When someone tried to challenge her intelligence, she used them as a weapon. Maria Antonia had good reason to rely on tales from her past. She grew up at a time when the automobile had not yet been invented. But she vividly recalled the first time she saw a Model-T Ford. During most of her childhood, radio and television were not yet a fixture in the tiny town of Muzquiz. That was the main reason she and her cousins spent their summers telling jokes and repeating wise Spanish sayings they had heard among their relatives.

She and her cousins were so close that she never imagined the revolution would send them in different directions.

She recalled how surprised she was to learn her cousin, Melecio Menchaca, had left Mexico years before she and her husband had crossed the border. Years later, she heard he had married a neighbor's daughter and settled in Chicago. The couple had five children, but Melecio's wife left him and returned to Mexico when the youngest was ten.

WHEN MARIA ANTONIA was transferred from Texas to Michigan, Gina began taking Minerva to visit Maria Antonia. Since Minerva had taken her adopted child to Michigan and had turned the boy over to Gina when she finally admitted she was too old and sick to keep him. Thereafter, Minerva admitted that because of her old age and chronic diabetes issues she could not care for the mischievous toddler. Predictably, she persuaded her daughter and son-in-law to raise him as their own.

Maria Antonia was a forgiving soul who was loyal to those she loved regardless of their transgressions. A perfect example was Minerva. Instead of being angry with her for leaving Texas before learning her fate at the Frankenmuth nursing home, she received her with open arms.

"Hija mia! ¿Dónde estabas? ¿Qué te paso? ¿Porque te fuiste?" Maria Antonia exclaimed. "Where have you been? What happened to you? Why did you leave?" Her queries and opened arms humbled her daughter, and ignoring her questions, she remained characteristically evasive.

Minerva was good at dodging questions that made her uncomfortable. She simply didn't answer. Then she'd strike up a conversation so off-the-subject and irrelevant that it left more than one family member wondering about her state of mind. Some family members said she was scatter brained and flighty. Others said she seemed distant and lost in thought during a conversation. But most criticism steered clear of any suggestion that there was something mentally wrong with her. If she suffered from any mental illness throughout her life, Maria Antonia didn't know it. She had always said her daughter was a dreamer. She blamed her inability to face reality as the reason for her first failed marriage.

Minerva's oldest daughters thought their mother was eccentric. She had demonstrated time and again her disregard for accepted social standards. She was the bohemian with a devil may care attitude that dominated her life.

It was not until Anita became a mother herself that she realized her mother had given birth to six children without ever feeling about them the way she felt about her own first-born child. Looking down at her infant son in her arms, Anita vowed her love for her son would always supersede any other love.

Despite this epiphany, Anita respected her mother. She never felt hatred or resentment toward her. She simply never understood why she had never shown her love. Unlike Anita, Mercedes López was resentful: "I didn't ask to be born!" she would exclaim when angry. Martha shared that she felt unloved and was verbally abused by their mother growing up.

> Mom doesn't love us. Look at the way she treats us. She has called me India macuasa since I was a baby. She calls you güera because of your light skin, hazel eyes, and light brown hair. But she calls Mercedes galga, which we thought meant skinny. But I found out it's a greyhound dog! I know she doesn't love us.

Minerva did nothing to allay her daughter's feelings. She didn't reassure her of her love for her or any of the children. While Minerva may have grown up hearing unsavory nicknames people called their children, she only assigned traditional nicknames for the three youngest.

Minerva was an enigma. Gloria, her sister-in-law, admired her spirit and intelligence, while her other sister-in-law, Mary, looked at her with disdain. Neither Gloria nor Beto's wife, Mary, had ever questioned old norms and Mexican traditions. However, Minerva Castañeda Peña was determined to live life on her terms, ignoring criticisms. Once, Anita told her mother that the church did not believe in divorce. Minerva became defensive and replied, "if movie stars are free to divorce so am I." Friends and family always thought it was odd that Minerva compared herself with Hollywood actresses instead of her own peers. When her children were youngsters, they didn't notice their mother was vastly different from the mothers of their friends. But in many respects, she was ahead of her times. She would tell her three oldest daughters:

> You must see yourself as you want to be seen, not as you are. You must aspire to have the very best. You must envision that you are an individual capable of achieving anything your mind desires. The riches of the entire world await those who want to succeed.

She begrudged that,

> Toña could never see that she didn't have to take us out of school each season to work in the fields. If she had not done that, I might have graduated from high school. I might have even gone to college.

Minerva Castañeda Peña admitted, "I was a bookworm. I used to sit among the cotton fields and read while Toña and my brothers worked." Minerva was an eighth-grade dropout. She was born too soon for the society in which she lived. A liberated woman long before news account heralded the burning of bras by women in the late 1960s, Minerva was a genuine "free spirit" until her dying day. She didn't believe that only the rich had the right to earthly creature comforts. She said it was not wrong, as the Catholic Church taught, to want to be rich. She would buy play money and tape it to her bedroom door with scotch tape. Lip service was not enough, she demonstrated her theory. She would emphasize,

> Think of all the good you can do with money. You can help yourself, your family, your church. You can also help others. Money itself is not bad or sinful; it's the people who

have it who become sinful and greedy. That is why some say money is the root of all evil, but it's not.

While Mercedes, Martha, and Anita didn't have long warm conversations with Minerva about her views or theirs, they retained much of her philosophy. A philosophy that guided them from their teen years all the way through adulthood. A bona fide non-conformist, Minerva dressed as she saw fit. She encouraged her daughters to do the same. For example, she would see a new fashion style and remark, "nothing on earth could make me wear what didn't suit me." She detested fashion designers, pronouncing them haute couture fascists. Minerva often stated,

> You girls need to be individuals. Don't let designers or others dictate what you should wear. Just because something is deemed fashionable doesn't mean you should go buy it and wear it. That dress or whatever you buy may look silly in public or ridiculous on you.

Most of her pronouncements came while her six children were young, but those assertions continued as they became teenagers and young adults. Anita was especially taken aback when she heard her mother say she would never be caught dead in blue jeans.

> When we did fieldwork, we all wore blue jeans. The material was tough enough to protect us during rigorous work. Nobody wore blue jeans except farmers and farmworkers. I used to tear those ugly jeans off as soon as we finished harvesting. And look at people now; they think they're fashionable wearing those things!

An advocate for higher education for her children, Minerva loved playing the role of a teacher. She seemed to prefer that to being physically affectionate with them. In fact, she once commented that it was her children who should kiss or embrace her, not the other way around! She had grown up without the affection of a father. And, while she never complained about lack of physical affection from her brothers or Maria Antonia, her children had seen her shower their stepfather and boyfriends with physical affection.

Mercedes, Martha, and Anita hated to see their mother beaming with happiness when she first started dating Mr. Ford. She would greet him with hugs and kisses. This was a slap in the face to three girls who never received displays of affection. Shortly after she became a widow, Mr. Ford was her focus. When confronted by Martha about it, Minerva said paying the bills and sharing her knowledge on things proved she cared for them as much as a mother who showed her love physically, saying,

> Toña hugs and kisses everybody! She kisses and hugs strangers but she's just your grandmother! I show I care through my actions. I buy your clothes and pay electricity, food, and water. I also teach you about many things through my knowledge.

Minerva loved playing the role of a wise, learned teacher, quizzing her children on Mexican history, American history, Spain's history, Texas history, geography, inventors, and great classical composers. Unlike Maria Antonia, who had only attended elementary school, and who never learned to speak English, Minerva had learned English in Dallas public schools. By age twelve, she'd mastered both languages, but always said Spanish was her first language.

When Minerva became a war bride and found it necessary to communicate with her non-English speaking mother-in-law, she recognized the importance of knowing two languages. The value of being bilingual was ignored by Texas public schools, where children were punished for speaking Spanish. She elaborated, "When I was a child attending school in Dallas, the teacher would punish any child they heard speaking Spanish. The teachers made Mexican children feel ashamed of their ethnicity and language."

From her, Anita learned that while the United States called itself a "melting pot," referring to America as a nation of immigrants, perpetuating an all-inclusive image. It told the world, via the Statue of Liberty in New York, that the huddled masses had arrived by the thousands because they yearned to be free. The reality was quite a shock to the descendants of the Mexican diaspora, even before the outbreak of the 1910 Mexican Revolution, Mexicans were repressed in every way. They had always been considered cheap labor, quasi slaves in the eyes of most people. Banning their spoken language in Texas schools was but one of a handful of institutionalized mandates as was control of their movement and their labor, along with insults. Minerva recalled being silenced and told her children,

> I was a quiet little girl who lived in fear of speaking up when I didn't like something. If I knew the answer to a teacher's question, I was afraid to raise my hand. In those days, Anglo teachers didn't think Mexican children were smart enough to know the answer.

Minerva would expand her point speaking to the reality of her educational experience. She critiqued educational practices and told them,

> We could not speak Spanish during recess or in school. We spoke Spanish at home and English at school. What was wrong with our language? Who did we hurt by speaking to each other in Spanish? I was very angry growing up. Why did we have to endure so much humiliation?

Then, when she gave birth to Mercedes, she resolved to challenge the Texas school system. She would not only teach her daughter Spanish, but it would be Spanish by-the-book. Toward that end, she bought Spanish-language books and began teaching her first-born child. As the other children arrived, the Spanish language was the only language allowed in her humble home.

The three fathers of her children were Mexican. Their native language was Spanish, making her job easier to accomplish for several years. Maria Antonia, who despite her daughter's denials helped raise her first three daughters, spoke broken English. This helped her establish and reinforce speaking Spanish even more.

Her three oldest daughters listened to what Minerva would tell them about Texas-style racial discrimination, as she spoke about the water fountains signs that read: "Negro" and "White," emphasizing that a Mexican child growing up in Texas never would forget this institutional segregation system.

She told them she ignored the signs and drank from both Dallas water fountains. She questioned how such segregation could exist in a country that proclaimed to be free and democratic, reminding them that Abraham Lincoln had freed the slaves and wondered if they felt free.

Racial discrimination was not limited to Texas. Michigan doled out its own brand of systemic oppression. In the 1940s when many Mexicans arrived, they populated the farms as agricultural workers. Anita was born in a small German and Polish enclave that would become multicultural decades later.

Maria Antonia arrived with her youngest son, her daughter and baby Mercedes to a town that made it clear they were not welcome. Minerva translated a sign that was on many of Saginaw's apartment buildings: "No Dogs, No Negroes, and No Mexicans." Maria Antonia was incredulous. She couldn't believe Mexicans could be treated in the same humiliating way as Negroes. She didn't realize until that first day in Saginaw, Michigan, that migrant workers usually didn't read these signs. Minerva told her daughters,

> Mexico abolished slavery long before Texas was stolen by the Anglo Southerners who brought their slaves with them to Texas. The slave owners wanted to keep slavery going, so they holed up in the San Antonio de Valero Spanish mission—what would later be called the Alamo—and started war with Mexico.

In her own way she taught an alternative history to her children. Minerva emphasized that,

> More than half of the United States used to belong to our forefathers. First it was under the Spanish flag, and, when Mexico gained its independence, it came under the Mex-

ican flag. Yet, we are now treated as foreigners in our own land. We are treated the same way they treated Negroes.

She believed that farmers were subtle in discriminating because they needed the cheapest labor they could find. The living quarters, however, spoke volumes. They were dilapidated shacks with no running water. The bathroom was an outhouse and farmers kept their distance unless they had more work for Mexicans to do their harvest.

By the time Minerva had her first child, she had read more than a dozen books on the history of Spain, Mexico, and the United States. Often, she would tell her children that knowledge was power. She urged them to defend their ideals, by especially reading history. There were also many newcomers to Michigan who had arrived directly from Mexico as World War II raged on. The ones who had arrived through the well-known Bracero Program as quasi-indentured servants, wanted more opportunities.

Minerva was a born teacher. Put another way, she was a teacher at heart. She often said that she didn't know where she inherited her love of reading, but she was certain it was not from her mother. She found willing students to inspire her among myriad Mexican immigrants who began populating German-dominated Saginaw. Mexico has not been a country that invests in its poorest citizens. And many of those who immigrated to the United States lacked a formal education. There were some who were impressed with her vast knowledge and sought her out. Once she formed a family with her third husband, she resolved to begin searching for her place in Michigan's expanding Mexican community.

Since she had sworn neither she nor her children would ever stoop to backbreaking agricultural work, Minerva, took a job at a local bakery. Unfortunately, picking cotton, tomatoes, potatoes and other crops had not prepared her for a job of operating a cash register.

When she told the manager she had worked at a Dallas-based airline, he hired her on the spot. Although he quizzed her on what she had done at the airline, he didn't think cleaning out airplanes for departing Braniff Airlines passengers would prevent her from learning to be a cashier. If she embraced the importance of arriving on schedule, she would have remained at that job. But she found an excuse for quitting, and Minerva would complain against time constraints and limitations.

> I had a home in Dallas while Manuel was at war. To work,
> I put little Mercedes in a nursery. We were happy while
> waiting for Manuel to come home. But Toña lured me to
> Michigan, and that was my downfall.

Minerva's lifelong trouble was not her ability to learn a new task, such as handling a cash register, rather Minerva did not live by a clock. Try as she may, Minerva was always late at any job that required being on time. Unable to fulfill this work requirement, she always lost the job. In typical fashion she would say she was destined for a higher position than being a cashier. Minerva saw herself as someone special. As someone who was endowed by God with a free will, foresight, ambition, and a drive that went beyond mundane accomplishments.

Maria Antonia berated Manuel Castañeda for being too lazy to keep a job. But her daughter believed he was an intellectual who refused to work as if he were a pack mule. Most likely Minerva inherited her love of reading and hunger for knowledge from her father. Minerva said,

> My mother, Toña, is illiterate. She never aspired for a bet-
> ter life. She always wanted to work and make money. She
> just worried about food and shelter but never tried reach-
> ing higher goals. We all can achieve higher positions in
> life, so I never agreed with her.

Minerva surprised her family by returning to school, but not to get a General Education Diploma but to become a hair stylist. Thus, after her journey to California and sale of her home in Saginaw, she enrolled in a cosmetology course.

Not having graduated from high school, because she was frequently absent due to her mother's commitment to migratory fieldwork, Minerva shocked her children, as well as her family, with the news she had scored higher than anyone in her class each time they were tested. Cosmetology courses required the study of the human body, the cells, the skin and several other areas. When she spoke about what she was learning it was as if her children were having a biology class in their own home. Maria Antonia applauded her thinking. She had finally found her true calling. She never tired of reciting what she'd read in her cosmetology lessons.

"What do you know about your red blood cells? Do you know too much exposure to the sun will rob your body of natural oils you can never replenish?"

"Do you know smoking ages your skin?"

"How many bones are in your body?"

Because she was brought up speaking Spanish in the home with her mother and her brothers, Minerva upheld the tradition of speaking Spanish with her own children. However, she began expressing herself more and more in English, once her children were grown!

When Minerva Castañeda Peña embarked on this educational journey, Mercedes was at Michigan State University on an academic scholarship, Martha was a seventeen-year-old grieving the death of her Irish American fiancé, and Anita was entering ninth grade. More importantly, for the first time in her life, Minerva had no Spanish-speaking husband or boyfriend. Becoming a widow had allowed her the freedom to explore new opportunities. Too busy to enforce her own rules, Minerva allowed the English language to finally take over her household.

When Minerva opened her beauty shop in the small town of Bay City, Michigan, Maria Antonia had moved away from her son Jeorge and his family. Proud, angry, and convinced she could go it alone despite her advanced age, Maria Antonia relocated briefly to California.

Minerva's solitude didn't last long. Soon she began longing for romance. Since she had stayed in touch with Mr. Ford before and after the California journey, they soon began dating. Shortly after, he persuaded her to sell her home and beauty shop and move to Midland, closer to where he lived.

One day she told her mother, "Compre terreno en Midland, y Señor Ford me hará una casa."

Maria Antonia responded, "Midland? ¡Eso es muy lejos!"

Unable to pronounce Midland, Maria Antonia gasped and followed by saying it was too far. "¿Por qué quiere hacerte casa allí? Why does he want to build you a house there?" Over the strong objections of her oldest daughters, Minerva uprooted her family and moved them to what could only be described as the wilderness. The three young children left fatherless by the death of her third husband, helped clear the land she had bought from Mr. Ford. While Mercedes remained in college unfettered by her mother's abrupt decision, Martha went searching for her father as a way of coping with the loss of her fiancée. That's why, upon high school graduation in 1962, she moved to Dallas.

Sixteen-year-old Anita fell into a deep depression. In her teen years, she hated being ripped from her city-centered environment. Maria Antonia still lived in the city with her son and his family, but Minerva refused to let her live with them to escape the life-altering move.

"Please let me go live with abuelita and Uncle Jeorge and Aunt Gloria! I promise to do good in school and graduate. We've never lived out in the country. From what I've seen, I'm not going to like it," Anita told her mother. Minerva replied,

> No! You are not going to live with Toña! She spoiled Martha to the point that she does whatever she wants. And I am not going to let her spoil you too. Until you are grown up, you belong here with us!

Mr. Ford ruled Minerva's life with an iron fist. Although he didn't move into the home he single-handedly built, his strict orders were followed as if he were Minerva's legal husband and stepfather to her remaining younger children. Among his cruelest edicts was the abolishment of an indoor bathroom. Since he thought himself a "naturalist," there was no need for electricity. Intended to be the sole source of heat during frigid Michigan winters was the wood-burning fireplace he had built. Well water was acceptable, although it took months for him to find and dig a well on the property.

Minerva behaved as if he was her first boyfriend. She would look at him coyly, and then simply gave in to his demands. When he was working as a home builder and woodcutter, Minerva would revert to being the kind of woman who meant business. She would order,

> Julián, bring in some wood every day before Mr. Ford gets here. He chopped it up so you must bring it in. Put it in the fireplace so we can burn it tonight to keep the house and ourselves warm.

Then, she added, "You girls need to get water from our neighbor until he digs a well." For Anita, the move was traumatic. She spent the next year crying and yearning to return to city life.

MARTHA WAS SMITTEN as soon as she arrived in Dallas. Her long-lost father had met Minerva here. When she called her sister with the exciting news, Mercedes began visualizing the last time she had seen him. However, she focused on school, instead of meeting her father or traveling far from home.

Manuel knew he only had two daughters. As promised, he followed up with a phone call to his former wife. As agreed, when Manuel called, he persuaded Minerva to allow his oldest daughter to travel to see him. He had also known for years that Anita carried his surname.

He called Minnie—the nickname he had given Minerva—and said,

> Minnie, this is your ex-husband, Manuel. Martha came to visit and plans to stay. I called Mercedes at your mother's house and asked her to come visit. It's been many years,

and I want to get to know my daughters. Mercedes asked me if Anita could come too. If you give her permission, it's okay with me.

Anita never intended to remain in Dallas permanently, but that's what happened. After three weeks of living under the same roof with her two oldest sisters, and their biological father, the trio hatched a plan that sealed the fate of teenage Anita. Manuel continued the conversation.

Minnie, I'm calling to tell you I'm planning to stay and work in Dallas. Mercedes, Martha, and Anita would like to stay here permanently. Anita is sixteen now and she doesn't want to go back to Michigan. If you give her permission to stay, I will be responsible for her as well as for Mercedes and Martha.

Minerva had always kept a closer eye on Anita. She knew how unhappy she had been since Mr. Ford persuaded her to move to Midland. At first, Minerva rejected the idea and worried that her daughter would not finish high school. When Manuel López promised to make sure Anita graduated, Minerva relented.

He reminded Minerva that he was the executive chef at a major Dallas hotel, and that he would pay the rent and utilities. So, by the end of their telephone conversation, Minerva had consented to let Anita finish high school in Texas.

Unfortunately, Manuel López's plan fell apart. Martha began violating her father's midnight curfews. Mercedes accepted a job at Neiman-Marcus but quit a month later. A letter confirming an extension of her four-year scholarship at Michigan State University sent Mercedes packing.

After high school graduation, Anita began attending a college in downtown Dallas. She met and eventually married Vicente Mas at the same time he enlisted in the U.S. Air Force. Stationed in two different bases during a four-year stint, the couple lived together until he decided to attend college.

After Maria Antonia left Jeorge's home, she found work in Los Angeles. But the job was short-lived when an earthquake jolted her back to Michigan. The night she landed at the airport a blizzard forced the cancelation of most flights. The only transportation available was a snow mobile. Despite her "broken" English she hired a driver at the airport to spirit her to her daughter's rural home in the snow.

The three younger children told and retold the story of the way Maria Antonia had departed Tri-City Airport amid a blizzard. When the entire city was paralyzed and flights had been canceled, Maria Antonia had paid a hefty sum to be taken to her daughter's home on a snow mobile.

"What? Grandma is coming back to Michigan? I don't believe it!" Anita exclaimed when her mother told her on the telephone. Minerva reminded her that Maria Antonia had always been a fearless woman, unafraid of anything, but the earthquake had sent her packing. She vowed never to return to California.

When Maria Antonia returned to Michigan, Minerva had stopped gazing into Mr. Ford's eyes. In fact, she had banished him from her home, telling her mother Mr. Ford had fallen into ill health because of prostate cancer. Although Maria Antonia never liked him, she was sympathetic. Maria Antonia had heard of Mr. Ford, long before she left her son's home, and moved away to work in California. She frowned on her daughter's decision to move to rural Midland. And when she heard about Mr. Ford's peculiar demands, she was outraged. "¿Qué tiene ese hombre? What's wrong with that man? ¿Qué no sabe que estamos en tiempos modernos? Doesn't he know we're in modern times? ¿Quién tiene escusado afuera? Who has an outhouse?" She shook her head in disbelief to hear there was no inside toilet in her daughter's home.

Throughout her life Minerva had demonstrated that the love of a man could propel her into a state of submissiveness beyond reason. She never hesitated to justify her actions by proclaiming love knew no boundaries. Her definition of love excluded any consideration for the feelings of her children. However, in the eyes of her three oldest children, their mother was a narcissist who confused sex with love. They were sure she was obsessed with romance. Of course, they arrived at this conclusion one day when they found a book tucked away in her chest of drawers, albeit they kept their perceptions secret.

"I think mom confuses love with sex. Look at this book," Martha told her sisters during their mother's early relationship with Mr. Ford. Mercedes cringed at the title: "The Art of Love." When she showed the book to fourteen-year-old Anita, she grabbed it. She began turning the pages and said,

> Mom always talks about love poetically. She says when you love someone anything goes. She says love means having a man no matter what. I can't believe she reads about love at her age! She's had three husbands! She's not officially married to Mr. Ford, but he might as well be her fourth!

Martha was ahead of both sisters regarding her understanding of love and sex. She said some of the books talked about love in physical terms. Since all her books came from the library, her mother didn't realize some had piqued her curiosity in areas she would have frowned upon. Martha told her visibly astonished sisters,

> Some of the books I've read talk about sex and say it's a normal part of living. Most people are going to be fulfilled by it when they fall in love. In fact, some authors say loving a man is life-altering. Other authors compare it to one's necessities. Falling in love is part of nature and at some point, we may experience it, and we must have it.

Mercedes wanted to tell their mother they had found the book. However, they would all be punished for looking in her chest of drawers. That's about the time Mercedes López begun telling the family she wanted to join a convent. Now she felt shame and guilt she'd seen such a book.

At fourteen, Anita was a tomboy. She was not yet interested in boys. Martha laughed at her genuine innocence. One day she told her to stop climbing trees, playing baseball, and pretending to be a tough cop. She insisted she shed that tomboy image and start paying more attention to boys.

Despite her insistence, Anita was in no hurry to become an adult. She ran when a boy tried to get close. If a boy caught her eye, she would daydream about him rather than try to get his attention. But things changed when she and her sister visited Manuel López.

She didn't know the trip to New Mexico would result in a road trip to Dallas, where she would live for the next three years and meet Vicente Mas. She could not have guessed he would agree to return with her to Michigan, to pursue a college degree.

When the news that not only had Martha left for Dallas, but that Mercedes and Anita had also left, Maria Antonia was overcome with worry and grief. The more she thought about it, the more her grief turned to anger about how negligent Minerva had been while raising them. She thought, wringing her wrinkled hands,

> All the years the girls were growing up I tried to help Minerva. I wanted the girls to be safe, well-fed, and cared for. Now they have all left home! Minerva never valued her girls! She always thought about herself, her needs and desires. My beautiful granddaughters are gone now.

Sometimes, try as she may, Maria Antonia could not help but criticize Minerva's impulsive decisions—she exasperated her. As Mercedes, Martha, and Anita matured, they concluded that their grandmother was the self-sacrificing, stable, and reasonable woman in their family.

As luck would have it, all three of Maria Antonia's oldest and closest granddaughters would return to Michigan for distinct reasons and at different times. Mercedes was the first one to return, after receiving a letter confirming the extension of her merit-based scholarship, which held the promise of a college degree.

Next, Anita would return as a married woman and young mother willing to work while her husband attended a local university on a full-time basis. The last one to return to Michigan, although only for a few months, was Martha.

Maria Antonia was at peace knowing her granddaughters had returned. But she wasn't aware that Martha had started dabbling in drugs. At the height of the social revolution of the 1960s, she had noticed significant changes in her precious granddaughter's personality. While both mother and grandmother interpreted her mood swings as part of her lifelong rebellious nature, they never guessed she had tried more than marijuana, a "weed" perceived as a steppingstone to much more lethal drugs.

Anita worked a full-time job as a bank teller while her husband, Vicente Mas, studied for a degree in computer science. As his graduation approached, he began to insist they move back to Texas. Why Texas? Vicente Mas had read a Time magazine article about Dallas being in the forefront of the emerging computer industry. Vicente and Anita had met while she lived with her sisters and their biological father Manuel López in Dallas.

Since Minerva felt her three youngest children were of age to fend for themselves, she began coaxing her mother to move back to Texas. They had spent decades living in frigid Michigan. Neither one wanted to continue shoveling snow. Now it was time for the two women to enjoy hot Texas weather. The move would also be an ideal way to get a fresh start and forget about Mr. Ford, Minerva thought. Maria Antonia's arthritis could also benefit from warmer weather, Minerva told her mother.

One day after a heated argument with Minerva, Martha swore she would not stay in boring Michigan. She took her clothes, informing her she was going to live with her aunt, uncle Jeorge and grandmother. This was less than an hour from Minerva's rural home. Maria Antonia received Martha with open arms, when she moved in uninvited.

Minerva told her mother, "She's twenty-one now; I can't tell her anything. I can't control her! I always knew she was just like her aunt Laura! I've had six children and she's the only one who always gave me trouble."

However, the family home Maria Antonia had bought, when her sons were at war, sold shortly after Martha moved in. With his share of the proceeds from the sale of the house, Jeorge had bought ten acres, while Maria Antonia had put hers in a saving account.

Several months after moving out to the farm, Maria Antonia had a disagreement with her son and his wife. She moved out at the same time Martha Lopez had moved in saying she could not live out in the boondocks after having lived in a glamorous city like Dallas. Surprisingly, instead of returning to Dallas, Martha said she was moving to Detroit, to live with a couple who had invited her to stay with them. She saw nothing wrong with that and always pushed the envelope with her attitude.

Martha loved flirting, smoking, and drinking. "I'm the 'black sheep' of the family," she proudly would say. But Anita López knew deep inside her sister was hurting. From the time she was a child, Martha had felt verbally abused and unloved by their mother. All three older girls had been whipped with a leather belt. And the tomboy may have deserved the ten lashes her mother doled out on occasion. But Anita did not think Mercedes, obedient, pious and unassuming, should ever get a beating.

In Anita's eyes, her oldest sister was as much of a saint as those she had read about in school. Mercedes always obeyed Minerva's constant demands: wash the dishes, scrub that floor, change that diaper, prepare the baby formula. Robbed of her childhood, she only found solace in education.

If Mercedes failed to do whatever task had been shoved at her, her mother used the leather belt. One day, though, she used a broom stick on Mercedes. Despite this abusive upbringing, she excelled in her studies. Mercedes was the first one to graduate from high school in the family, and graduated summa cum laude.

Martha, by comparison, challenged licks from the leather belt. She had taken up smoking cigarettes at the age of thirteen. She had no fear of boys. One night she got into the car of a school friend without permission. Later, she was dumped on the front porch of her home totally drunk. Martha was a fearless creature who was willing to try most anything. She was the one who challenged her strict Catholic school rules. A breach concerning her school uniform led the principal to discover a pack of cigarettes and sleeping pills in her purse.

"La India macuasa is in trouble again at school," Minerva shouted, referring to her daughter's hair, eyes and cinnamon-colored skin. Any relative who heard the nickname for Martha knew it was derogatory and that it carried the impact of making anyone feel inferior. Maria Antonia was the first to loudly object, telling Minerva not to give the girls sobrenombres or nicknames, especially unflattering ones. Maria Antonia told her daughter, shaking her head in disgust, "¡Válgame Dios!" Maria Antonia exclaimed the day she heard her daughter call Martha India macuasa. "¿Qué importa si tiene raza india? Tú también la tienes. So, what if she's Indian, so are you."

Minerva, you should not call my little Mercedes and Martha such awful names. ¿Qué importa? Who cares if Martha looks more Indian than Spanish? We all have Indian blood! You should not call Mercedes la galga or greyhound dog either.

Anita had the best nickname of the three. She was called güera, in reference to someone with light-colored skin. She knew her skin color was lighter because of her father, but she loved Mercedes and Martha as if they were her full-blooded sisters. Still, she worried her older sisters would grow up to resent her because her nickname conjured a more acceptable and positive image, including lighter hair and hazel eyes like her father Jesús Sosa. Minerva told Anita López on one of those rare occasions she talked about the men in her life, that he was the only man she had ever loved. "Your father was often mistaken for a German instead of Mexican."

Anita loved her sisters as much as she loved the three youngest children from her mother's third marriage. Even before her mother was widowed, she had helped feed and take care of them. She felt so responsible for them, she often felt as if she was their mother.

The youngest children left fatherless by the untimely death of Ricardo Peña also loved and looked up to the oldest sisters. Like most children of a single mother, they were powerless to change the course of their lives until they reached adulthood.

Maria Antonia had spent half her life helping her son and his family in Michigan. Now, it seemed as if the stars had aligned to ensure that part of the family remained together. While Minerva was trying to persuade her mother to move to Texas, she got a telephone call from a hospital in Detroit. "We are calling from the psychiatric department at Detroit Methodist Hospital. Do you have a daughter by the name of Martha López?" the doctor asked. With a furrowed brow, for a split second, Minerva hesitated before acknowledging that she had a daughter by that name. The doctor said, "We want to notify you that we found your daughter lying on a street here in Detroit. We believe she needs psychiatric treatment. But we need you to come and sign papers giving us permission to treat her."

MARIA ANTONIA was shocked when Minerva told her Martha was in trouble, and she must immediately leave for Detroit. As usual, Minerva did not have money to drive from Saginaw to Detroit. However, upon hearing that her granddaughter was in a hospital, Maria Antonia instantly produced a wad of twenty-dollar bills. They agreed to form a partnership in pursuit of her cure. "Toma, gasta lo que necesites, pero tráela para la casa." María Antonia handed a wad of money to Minerva, telling her, "Spend what is necessary but bring Martha home. Aquí entre tú y yo la curamos."

Anita stopped working six months before her husband, Vicente Mas, graduated. She had given birth to a second child and chose to start a nursery to supplement her full-time income. Moreover, it was time to think about the future and consider the big move back to Dallas. Anita, Vicente and their children had lived two hours from Maria Antonia and her mother, while Vicente Mas finished his degree. But it was not until several years passed that she heard the harrowing account of the way in which Minerva had freed Martha from a Detroit hospital for the mentally ill. Minerva recalled,

When we got to the Detroit hospital, the building looked more like a prison! Thank goodness the kids went with me. They saw Martha locked up in what looked like a dungeon. Gina cried while the others stood in shock. My heart ached for Martha. How could my daughter have ended up here?

Anita could not believe what her mother was telling her about the condition in which they had found her sister. She added that it was bad enough that Martha had dabbled in marijuana and LSD but that the doctor assigned to her case had prescribed additional drugs.

Minerva yelled, when recounting the ordeal, "that crazy doctor gave Martha a bagful of drugs! That is why I always say to stay away from doctors; they want to treat everything with dangerous drugs, instead of finding a cure" Minerva rejected more drugs as treatment for her daughter. Maria Antonia had brought her up to never place confidence in doctors or drugs and she raised her four children through a variety of childhood illnesses with nothing but prayers and a bevy of natural herbs and teas. Maria Antonia recalled that the only time a doctor had come to her rescue was when Jeorge had been deathly ill. So, in a rare instance where mother and daughter agreed, they resolved to cure Martha together.

Faced with the obligation of giving her consent so Martha could remain in the horrific hospital, she opted to take her daughter without the doctor's consent. As the mother of the patient, she reasoned that she had the final say about what kind of medical care her daughter should receive. While the nurse on duty slipped away to locate the doctor, Minerva dressed her daughter and half ran through the hospital corridor with her children in tow. Later, Minerva said she had never driven her 1962 Buick faster than that day.

With even greater urgency Maria Antonia withdrew all her life savings and cashed in her life insurance, convinced that it was indeed time to move to Texas. She came to this conclusion while helping her daughter deal with Martha's comatose state. For the first time in years, mother and daughter worked as a team to nurse Martha back to health. Thanks to Maria Antonia's gentle, loving bedside manner, Martha swallowed cup after cup of what seemed like gallons of lemon, ginger, chamomile, cinnamon, and hibiscus teas.

Minerva had always believed in the healing powers of vitamins and minerals. To that end, she gave her vitamin A, B12, C and selenium, magnesium, and other minerals. In two weeks, Martha slowly returned to her stubborn though guarded self again.

Minerva had discovered classical music while taking Martha and Anita to ballet lessons. She believed this extraordinary music had healing powers. Minerva often told her daughters she used to envision ballet dancing to classical music, while toiling in the cotton fields of Texas as a child. She told them she didn't dare tell her mother all about her dreams and future aspirations. She feared being ridiculed or punished for rejecting what her mother clearly saw as her ultimate destiny. Each time her mother caught her daydreaming, she'd ask her what she was thinking. But young Minerva remained quiet.

> Toña used to get after me in the cotton fields … saying "Look at your brothers! Look how much cotton they've picked and you're just sitting there! You need to help us work or we won't have a roof over our heads and enough food to eat." I was daydreaming, wearing a tutu and black ballet slippers, I saw myself leaping into the air.

Her resentment against Maria Antonia was palpable, although not something she had ever talked about, Minerva would tell her daughters. "My mother didn't try to find work in Dallas or another city. I hated that I didn't go to school all year round like other children. And I hated doing migrant work—it's like child slave labor."

In hopes of helping Martha heal mentally, Minerva played Beethoven, Bach, Mozart and the music of other classical composers. Yet the most heart-wrenching difference mother and grandmother noticed was that for no apparent reason Martha wept continuously, while the music played on.

Fate stretched out its benevolent hand so that Maria Antonia, Minerva, Martha, and Eva Peña spent the first twelve months in Austin. The idea was to give Martha the opportunity she wanted at the local university. With that in mind, Maria Antonia and her daughter had to delay beginning their life anew in San Antonio.

Mr. Ford had built Minerva Castañeda Peña a house on the five acres he had sold her in rural Michigan, and she left the house to her only son, Julián Peña. Gina would marry the boy next door in a few weeks. Martha would return to Texas, and Eva Peña, her youngest, simply went along not knowing what to expect. Shy, seventeen-year-old Eva would say years later that she had no choice but to move with her mother and grandmother. Her father had died when she was a toddler. She never knew him except for a black-and-white picture taken while dating her mother, Minerva. With her biological sister on the brink of marriage, and her only brother relegated to odd jobs after high school graduation, Eva Peña saw no reason to remain in the two-bedroom house where she'd grown up without an indoor bathroom.

Martha López, Minerva Castañeda Peña, and Eva Peña had no money to journey by car from Michigan to Texas. Maria Antonia told them not to worry. She said she had plenty of money for travel expenses, rent for the first month, and a down payment on a house in San Antonio. Still, the road to Texas was paved with strife. Martha wanted to stay in Austin. She had read the University of Austin offered a degree in television and film studies. Despite her harrowing brush with mental illness facilities in Detroit, she was convinced she could get a job and attend college classes. Maria Antonia said she had fed and diapered her, Mercedes and Anita since birth. And she did not want to see her alone in a strange city. Each time Minerva heard Maria Antonia say this she'd go into a rage accusing her mother of emotional kidnapping, and Maria Antonia countered,

You took Anita and went to live with Jesús in Montana. You left the girls with strangers. When I found out, I went to the babysitter and told her I was the grandmother. Beto and I took them with us to work during cherry picking season in Traverse City, Michigan.

Maria Antonia was so close to her three granddaughters she would have done anything for them. Predictably, she could not fathom leaving Martha alone in a new city. Their initial reluctance gave way to all four women agreeing to rent an apartment in Austin. Although Maria Antonia and her daughter preferred to continue to San Antonio, they were willing to delay their plans until Martha was well enough to consider her future.

Once cleared by a local doctor and put on prescription medication she enrolled at the local university. Martha López insisted, "I'm not sick anymore. The doctor gave me medicine so that I can work and live alone. I qualify for grants and maybe even a scholarship. So, you, abuelita, and Eva can go on and leave me here." In the end, and to keep the peace, Maria Antonia remained in Austin, while her daughter and granddaughter, Eva, went on to San Antonio to rent a house until she felt sure Martha would be well enough to live alone.

Predictably, Martha reverted to her bad habits. She pursued the lost generation of Americans who found comfort in mind-bending drugs. She consumed wine and all forms of alcoholic beverages. She dabbled in art instead of following an official, counselor-approved curriculum aimed at culminating in a college degree. Martha was smart, but she always chose bad over good. She was not only a bookworm who had read and amassed a thousand books, she was a gifted ballet dancer. In fact, she had outperformed her own teacher. Despite bleeding toes, she executed difficult steps in such traditional ballets as Swan Lake and the Nutcracker.

Anita admired her older sister so much she never thought her example could lead to her own corruption. She loved her sister unconditionally, which blinded her from seeing Martha's insane jealous, self-destructive personality. Anita concluded that Martha simply made poor, mindless choices. Anita López once told her aunt, Gloria, who was a wonderful attentive listener,

Martha isn't bad; she's just curious and impatient. Our mother has always told her to reach for the stars regardless of class or status. Martha learned about the world through the books she read and the performing arts. But none of the positive experiences could deter her self-destructive habits.

Following a year in Austin, Martha wanted to live alone. She said she had met the love of her life and would be moving in with him. Her mother received the news calmly while Maria Antonia seemed shocked. Still, neither one was going to continue to fight decisions made by Martha.

Soon after, Maria Antonia joined her daughter and Eva Peña determined on making San Antonio their home. They had rented a dilapidated house in a Spanish-speaking neighborhood south of downtown San Antonio. It was ten blocks from opulent homes built by wealthy German immigrants. Eva Peña didn't know a soul when she enrolled in San Antonio College. And being painfully shy, she didn't make friends quickly. Her mother, who had a knack for attracting men, soon had a new man in her life. That was the first red flag Eva saw, and the reason she began to regret her decision. Minerva's choice of men had always been a source of embarrassment for the family, including her children, the family had learned to grudgingly accept it. She would never have given up her choices had anyone asked her to do it for the sake of her children or her mother. Minerva Castañeda Peña would often say, if one of her daughters questioned her about her desire for a man,

> I don't live my life according to what others may say about it. This is my life to live the way I want to live it. Look at Marilyn Monroe, Judy Garland, Elizabeth Taylor! If they can marry so many times, so can I.

When Anita told Maria Antonia how Minerva defended her lifestyle choices, she said Minerva did not reflect her values. Moreover, Maria Antonia saw her daughter as being out of touch with reality for comparing herself to Hollywood movie stars.

A few months after living in the rented house, Minerva saw a for-sale sign in front of an old, condemned house. Maria Antonia said it looked like her house in Michigan. She paid eleven thousand dollars in cash, convinced that a good cleaning and repairs would make it livable. Mother and daughter were genuinely excited to start their lives anew in San Antonio. The weather was something they knew would be good for them. Since the home was on the south end of the city, they thought they would find cheap labor to begin restoring the old house.

Unfortunately, a call that spelled trouble came from an Austin hospital. This time, the doctor said Martha needed to go home within thirty days. She was referred to a local psychiatrist who diagnosed her as paranoid schizophrenic. Mother and daughter boarded the next Greyhound bus to Austin. After Martha was released from the hospital, Dale English, the young man she had met and moved in with, offered to take care of her. He said he loved her and would see her through this crisis. Still, Maria Antonia insisted on staying to help Martha recover. Maria Antonia told Minerva that she would be more helpful returning to the newly bought home in San Antonio and gave her $200 dollars to begin fixing a leak in the old roof.

Dale English did not speak a word of Spanish. Maria Antonia's English was limited. Yet the two got along beautifully during her six-month stay with the couple in Austin. Maria Antonia had trusted that her daughter would continue where they had left off in repairing the house. Reassured that Martha would regain normality if she stayed on prescription medication, Maria Antonia returned to San Antonio, only to find out that none of the repairs to the house had been made. Minerva had latched on to a new man. But most disappointing and distressing for Maria Antonia was that Minerva's gigolo boyfriend had been staying at the house rent-free, and that she forgot about the repairs. Of course, Maria Atonia called her out.

Minerva, I see you haven't done the repairs. It's raining outside and the roof still leaks. The windows need plastic to keep the cold air out. I gave you plenty of money. And the whole time I've been in Austin, I trusted you to get things done!

Minerva always had an excuse, regardless of how unreasonable it sounded. She said her 1962 Buick had broken down, so she was forced to fix it to get around. Then, she couldn't find a job. She even mentioned that Eva, her youngest, was no help because she was in college. Enraged, Maria Antonia would tell Anita on one of her many visits about Minerva's abuses.

> When I give your mother money to go buy food, she comes back with vitamins. She's unapologetic because she says we need them. Other times, she returns with rose bushes instead of food. Then I say, "Válgame Dios Minerva, we can't eat rose bushes!" But she's unapologetic, adding they were too beautiful to pass up.

Maria Antonia knew her daughter all too well. She tried not to say that she doubted her. But sooner or later she would confront her about her irresponsible spending. That would lead to one big, never-ending Spanish-language argument about her presence in Texas, saying "You would not be here in Texas were it not for me." Minerva would shout at Maria Antonia, saying, "I drove my car, paid for gas and moved you here. You wanted to move here. I had my home in Michigan bought and paid for. I didn't have to come to Texas!"

Of course, Minerva's daughters would have challenged what Minerva claimed. They would say it was not true. Truth be told, she had exhausted her credit worthiness to the point that not a single financial institution in Saginaw would loan her any money. What's more, she knew Maria Antonia had cashed in her life insurance and received her share from the sale of the large, two-story house she had bought in Saginaw while her son, Jeorge was ending his service in Korea as a paratrooper in the U.S. Army.

Unlike her mother, Minerva had never had a savings account long enough to do her any good. Each time she opened one, she made up some excuse to withdraw from it a little at a time until there was nothing left. She had struggled to manage money from the time she was young. Even with a $500 monthly social security income she ran out of money before her next check.

Because of the continued strife between Maria Antonia and Minerva, Eva Peña soon became so angry and depressed that she withdrew from her classes at San Antonio College. She called her sister, Gina, and told her she wanted to return to Michigan. Gina had gone through with her marriage to the boy next door and had officially become Gina Peña Schmidt. The newlyweds did not have a formal education beyond high school but their love for each other and faith gave them hope. They both managed to find work in the city. Luckily, a vacant mobile home on his parents' property became their permanent residence. The couple took pity on Eva and offered her their second bedroom in their modest home. Gina told her sister, Eva Peña,

> You can come and live with us if you want. The mobile home we're renting has a second bedroom. Julián still lives in mom's house. He hasn't fixed the stinky septic tank problem. If you want, you can live with him in mom's old house, too. But the stench is unbearable.

Of all Minerva's children, Julián Peña had fared worse. Since his biological father had died when he was just two years old, his mother's boyfriend, Mr. Ford, had been the only father figure he'd had growing up. When his mother left Michigan, Julián Peña went to work for a grocery store in the city. His meager paycheck paid for necessities like food and electricity. Well water and a wood burning fireplace helped him survive frigid winters. He didn't have money for anything else, including repair of the septic tank.

Long before Maria Antonia had moved out and away from the home she had shared with her son and his large family, Minerva had lacked the money to maintain the septic tank necessary to continue living in her rural home in the backwoods. Consequently, when she moved to Texas, the sewage had built up to the point that neighbors held their collective noses, cringing as they raced down the road, bent on avoiding the smell. Julián lived from paycheck to paycheck.

Tragically, he had no choice but to tolerate the stomach-turning stench indefinitely.

Although Maria Antonia's social security check was less than Minerva's, she always had money tucked away. That's why she gave Eva Peña fifty dollars for a one-way bus ticket back to Michigan, and she gave her an additional twenty, saying she'd need it for food during her two-day journey.

Eva Peña did not speak Spanish. She had grown up in rural Midland. Unlike her three older, half-sisters, she had not received Maria Antonia's physical warmth as an infant nor her spiritual guidance growing up. She was a five-year-old child when her mother, Minerva, moved her and her biological sister and brother to the boondocks. The three youngest of the six children would never know the city. Neither would they have the experience, and perhaps the benefit, of having a Roman Catholic education. Eva Peña would say,

> I never liked living out in the wilderness. When mom took us to live out there, we had to use a sickle to cut away the thick brush before she had the house built. In spring and summer, there were so many mosquitos, it was unbearable. That's why I always wanted to move to the city.

Michigan winters were unforgiving, and since her mother's house was heated with wood Mr. Ford had chopped into logs from the expansive forest, there were bitter cold nights when Eva Peña wet her bed. Not only was the firewood insufficient, but she was too cold to make tracks in the snow to the outhouse. It's no wonder that for years Eva fantasized about leaving Michigan. She had heard Martha talk about her first trip to Texas, and listened to her speak about the wonderous city of Dallas. She never expected her mother and grandmother to move to Texas.

That's why she joyously agreed to join her mother, grandmother, and half-sister knowing full well that disagreements, arguments, and bickering were bound to happen as they drove to the Lone Star State. When family members heard about young Eva moving to Texas, they predicted she'd return.

Taking the money from Maria Antonia, Eva Peña humbly said thank you in English. Then looking at her mother, she asked: "How do I say Thank You for also paying my college expenses?" Before she could reply, Maria Antonia hugged her and covered her face with kisses. She had a way of making anyone feel loved without saying a word.

Maria Antonia always seemed embarrassed when those on the receiving end of her generosity kissed her and tried to express their gratitude. To many family members she had helped and strangers as well, she said "it was nothing." She'd brush off thanks by saying: "No, No, No es nada; hoy tú, mañana yo. Today is for you and tomorrow may be for me." She strongly believed that charity begins at home by helping one's own family first. But she also felt strongly about feeding and helping everyone, regardless of race or color, along with God's creatures. Stray cats and dogs, birds, squirrels, and any manner of creature who appeared on the wide, wooden porch of Maria Antonia's two-story San Antonio home—they received generous portions of leftover food from her kitchen.

Situated on one third of an acre, her home had what she called a "casita" in the deepest part of the yard. Called a "granny flat" in English, the two-bedroom, one bath "casita" was also a source of income for Maria Antonia and her daughter. Low-income renters reaped the benefits of more than low rent. In her enormous backyard, dotted with pecan trees and two peach trees, she had started a colorful garden. With the help of Minerva, she planted okra, potatoes, tomatoes, corn, cilantro and all types of squash.

Thanks to Maria Antonia's generosity, and an abundant bounty, all renters received free fresh fruits and vegetables each season. Her love of flowers, plants and gardening was only exceeded by her love of animals. When creatures such as field mice, squirrels, armadillos and racoons invaded her garden, over the screams of her livid daughter, Maria Antonia merely said,

Pobrecitos, ellos también tienen hambre como nosotros. Poor little ones, they too get hungry like us. Tienen que comer como sea. They must eat however they can. Al fin y al cavo, son creaturas de Dios. After all, they are God's creatures.

Continuing in Spanish, she asked Minerva,

> Who am I to keep those poor animals from surviving? Aren't we all creatures of God? Didn't God say it is better to give than to receive? Everything we have on earth is temporary. We must not be so greedy as to ever deny anyone, human being or animal, the basic need for food.

Maria Antonia had also learned how to make red wine from table grapes. Her daughter recalled that her mother had made wine during the Great Depression. Minerva listened in amazement when Maria Antonia told her the yard in her San Antonio home was large enough to plant a few vines. Minerva Castañeda Peña recalled telling her mother,

> I remember how you used to make wine when we were growing up. You took table grapes and covered them up for several weeks, but I don't know if we can do that here in this city without a permit, and we are too old to pick them ourselves.

Maria Antonia said her aunts told her there was a town not far from Muzquiz where vineyards could be seen for miles. They cultivated grape varietals to make red wine. This was a legacy of the Spanish missionaries who had arrived in Mexico in the 1500s. Since Mexico did not commercialize wine to import to the United States and other countries, many Mexican people never knew how to make wine, nor did they work among vineyards. But Teofela and Enriqueta Menchaca knew all about winemaking. Maria Antonia recalled that her aunts were steeped in the winemaking tradition.

> They said winemaking was part of Spanish culture. Making wine and drinking it was in keeping with what Jesus Christ taught us. We had a taste each Sunday at Mass. They also enjoyed it as a beverage. They said drinking wine

would help me enter gracefully into society. But I wasn't as fond of drinking it as I was of learning how to make it.

With a laugh, Maria Antonia recalled that her female relatives were conservative, industrious ladies who knew how to do many things. They saw me at first as a wild child. They said being reared in a remote rancho by a widower resulted in my lack of grace, poise, and proper manners. They taught me everything I needed to know to go out in the world as a well-bred, proper young woman.

Sadly sighing, Maria Antonia recalled the tragic way in which her beloved aunts died. She said, "Estábamos en Dallas cuando me llego la carta de mi tío Fulgencio diciendo que habían muerto en un incendio. We lived in Dallas when I received a letter from uncle Fulgencio saying they had died in a fire." And no one knew how it had started.

MARIA ANTONIA lived to celebrate one hundred and six years of age in the Frankenmuth nursing home. She had been a celebrity from the day she arrived. Despite being the oldest-ever resident at the facility, residents and staffers alike quickly realized it was not just Maria Antonias age that inspired curiosity and admiration.

To visit her beloved abuelita, Anita flew from Dallas to Michigan. With a heavy heart during the flight to Michigan, she would review all the things she wanted to tell her. Each time she had to say goodbye, Anita was sure it would be the very last time she would see abuelita.

She had never stopped feeling guilty about the role she had played in having Maria Antonia transferred to Michigan. In agreement with a Texas court, her cousins, and their father, Jeorge Castañeda, they felt it was best for abuelita to live her remaining years near her three adult children. Martha moved from Austin to Tulsa with her devoted husband. Consequently, Anita became Maria Antonia's closest relative. And based on what she'd seen at the San Antonio nursing home, she was sure her grandmother would die from neglect. That's why she asked her uncle and cousins for help.

From the moment she arrived in Michigan, Maria Antonia's family was unwavering in their love and support for abuelita. Beto visited her three times a week. Assisted by his wife, and with help from Hilda who arranged weekly visits with the nursing home director, wheelchair-confined Jeorge Castañeda visited his mother.

Gina Peña Schmidt and Eva Peña, who married the son of a local home builder shortly after returning to Michigan, took Minerva to visit her mother each week. Minerva's failing health and limited vision had prevented her from obtaining a Michigan driver's license. The nursing home was unique in that it adopted several animals to interact with the residents. Everyone thought Maria Antonia would love that. But she questioned their displacement. "Why did the home bring them here? They don't want to be caged up in here anymore than I do!" Three bright red cardinals and a couple of long, slender parakeets were caged up in the lobby. The goal was to bring some joy to the residents. A small cocker spaniel with silky hair and droopy ears roamed around, to make them feel more cheerful.

For Maria Antonia the unorthodox program had the reverse effect. She pitied the birds for being caged, thereby preventing them from flying as God had intended. The dog reminded her of her own, making her nostalgic. She recalled how he had died shortly before she was forced from her home.

Near her final year in Frankenmuth, Maria Antonia finally stopped asking her daughter to get her out of the nursing home. She no longer asked her about the San Antonio house the two shared for so many years. During those final years as a nursing home resident, Hilda Zonlak organized Maria Antonia's 104th birthday party. Family members couldn't help but notice Maria Antonia had become more distant. On one visit, Anita found her quietly sitting in her wheelchair in a corner of the living room residents shared.

"Abuelita, ¿Por qué estás aquí sola? Grandma why are you here so alone," she asked, stroking her white hair. Apparently, she had wheeled herself into the tiny space, as if to deliberately isolate herself. Instead of her usual amiable face, abuelita now looked disheartened.

Anita attributed her alienation to the reality that not a single staffer spoke Spanish. That's why she had always stressed to family members that visiting Maria Antonia, who loved talking about her past, was very important.

Still, memories of her birthplace were vivid even as her spirited personality declined. Memories of surviving the Mexican Revolution never faded. She spoke lovingly of her prim and proper aunts, and how they had brought her up until she married Manuel Castañeda and left their home. Maria Antonia recalled,

> If I had paid more attention, I would've learned more about my own aunt's upbringing. I remember that they were very dignified ladies. The way they wore their hair pulled up in a bun; their table manners and their reluctance to ever shout, because shouting was for street vendors.

Because most of Maria Antonia's grandchildren and great-grandchildren didn't speak Spanish, they never learned as much as Anita López about how this amazing woman had survived the Mexican Revolution in a time of fear, famine, and certain death.

They would never have heard about the 1918 Spanish flu that killed many young Mexicans at a time when the whole country was still reeling from the ravages of the bloody revolution. Before her marriage at age seventeen, Maria Antonia recalled hearing about the deadly disease from visitors and locals who had traveled to the capital or read newspapers headlines about the circulating illness. She said,

> Muzquiz was no more than a village when that horrible flu hit us like the black plague. My aunts said we had to try staying indoors until it ended. Businessmen, including my uncles, scrubbed the stores and streets with

creolina, a strong disinfectant. Again, we prayed the rosary day and night.

Anita had heard it all. Maria Antonia had said her aunts were well-mannered and industrious. They had their own vegetable garden. They sewed and crocheted to earn money to buy what they couldn't grow themselves. Maria Antonia didn't hold minute details about them and often shared,

> I don't know exactly where they learned all the skills they had. They sang Spanish songs and played an old, upright piano they had. They were even artists and sculptors who made and painted ceramic objects that were functional and decorative, or both.

The creation of manual arts was another way she learned about culture and life in her pueblo. She said, "mis tías aunts taught me how to make piñatas; they taught me to make the papier mâché piñatas too. They earned pesetas from their handiwork." She never explained why her aunts always used the word "pesetas" instead of "pesos" as other Mexicans did when talking about money. The consequences of war were despicable. Maria Antonia said,

> In those horrible times food was so scarce people roamed around looking in trash cans. They knocked on doors asking for food or for a peseta. I learned from my aunts it was better to give than to receive, so I always felt pity for those less fortunate. We gave what little we had.

Not yet declared a city, those days Muzquiz was a village. It was a place where everyone knew each other. She remembered that "When the revolution began, many of us didn't take sides. We never dreamed the uprising would lead to the slaughter of more than a million of our own people." Later, "After Francisco Madero was assassinated by Victoriano Huerta, the man who replaced him, Venustiano Carranza, was also killed." During this tumultuous time in Mexico, my aunts talked about their fear. "Yet they said they did not want to leave their home and country." She said,

192

What we did instead was that when we heard gunfire or the hoofs of horses pounding in the distance, we simply hid underneath the house. We prayed to our lady of Guadalupe. She must have heard our prayers, because neither my aunts or I suffered the horrors of rape as other girls and women had.

The different factions would come into Muzquiz and update the residents on the revolution.

One day we would hear about the forces of Pancho Villa being victorious in the northern part of the country, and the next we would hear of Emiliano Zapata being triumphant in another part. We would also hear of brutal, bloody battles that made our blood run cold. As for me, I was just a young child being raised by two dignified "old maids" in a town caught in the middle of a revolution.

Maria Antonia added, "During those horrific times, I was always afraid for my father. When he appeared safely at the front door, I felt relieved to see him." Maria Antonia's father had great compassion for those who fought in the conflict.

My father used to tell his sisters and brothers that the revolution reflected the uprising of Mexico's poorest. And, he added, "The Revolution helped the rich get richer and politicians to gain more money and power."

In the end, innocent civilians always paid the price of war. For example, many children missed their education. Without shame and in her first language, Maria Antonia explained why she didn't receive a basic education.

You probably wonder why I didn't get a basic education. You don't know why I can only sign my name and write simple Spanish sentences. Well, during the revolution, the school wasn't always open, and the only schoolhouse near Muzquiz was a mile away.

She offered that poverty was also implicated in maintaining the illiteracy of the people. Maria Antonia explained,

> When you are worried about food and shelter, education is unimportant. My aunts, although quite refined, didn't insist I go to school. Much like my father, my aunts were self-sufficient. Their two-story house in Muzquiz was on several acres. They had cows, sheep, chickens, roosters and horses.

The way she saw it, Maria Antonia recognized that life experience provided her the knowledge to survive. She said,

> I learned more outside of school than I would have learned in school. I learned how to survive using my own ideas, intelligence, and talents. The handicrafts and things I learned from my aunts helped me navigate through waves of an uncertain future.

Daily chores in the ranch prepared her for marriage and to take on life as a survivor. She told Anita and whomever else in the family wanted to know:

> By the time I married your grandfather, I knew how to cook and sew, in addition to milking a cow, sheering sheep, and horseback riding. I had seen death in my town where people died from starvation, disease and war. That's why I strongly suggested to my husband, Manuel, we'd go to the United States.

Newspaper reports heralded the end of the Mexican Revolution in 1920. But the succession of presidential assassinations, including Madero, left Mexicans questioning the legitimacy of a new, democratic style of government. A decade of war had left the economy in shambles and the future was more uncertain than ever.

In 1924, Manuel Castañeda agreed with Maria Antonia's firmly held belief that their future was to be in the United States. He could not deny it held the most hope for the future of their children. Young and naïve, she envisioned an abundance of food, a new home, and work for Manuel as an accountant again.

Abuela would tell her granddaughters about the family's migration experience, continuing her lengthy journey through her past.

> Your mother was only nine months old when we crossed over from Mexico into the United States. Your uncle Paco was not yet of school age. Like other Mexican immigrants, we were not prevented from entering. We simply crossed the bridge in Laredo along with hundreds of other Mexicans seeking a new life.

Anita López never tired of hearing abuelita's stories about the revolution and the Great Depression, two of the most life-altering eras she had lived through. As the hours passed, the days and years in the Michigan nursing home, Maria Antonia began losing her indomitable spirit while retaining her mind.

This change in her grandmother's personality worried Anita. Aside from talking to her cousin about it, she was unable to do anything. When she boarded a flight from Texas to Michigan to visit abuelita, Anita usually stayed with her uncle Jeorge and his wife, Gloria.

Although Hilda Zonlak was busy bringing up three children, she remained the official guardian. Her ability to organize and attention to detail proved to be exactly what the family needed to ensure their abuela would be as healthy and happy as humanly possible.

Six months after Maria Antonia's relocation, Anita flew to Michigan to celebrate her grandmother's birthday. She recalled the excitement of her first visit. Close family members descended on Jeorge's sprawling rural home to welcome Maria Antonia back to the state where she had lived for decades. However, it was the birthday celebration when she reached the age of one hundred and four at the Frankenmuth nursing home that no one would soon forget. The unexpected letter from President George W. Bush and First Lady Laura Bush made the event extra special. Also, what made this birthday memorable was that everyone witnessed Maria

Antonia's great ability to discern between fact and fiction. Never having been a gullible person, abuelita had asked to see the official envelope to confirm the letter had really come from the White House. Her great intellect led her to question, not unreasonably, that a great and powerful person had taken the time to send her a birthday greeting. And that his equally important wife had joined him in their good wishes.

In addition to Maria Antonia's own speech, her sons, grandchildren, nieces, nephews and friends had something positive and interesting to say about her charismatic personality. Anita López was sure that if President George W. Bush and the First Lady Laura Bush had met Maria Antonia, they would have been more amazed by her sharp mind.

Even with limited English skills, Maria Antonia always said what was on her mind. She had defended the American flag like a true patriot. She had blessed her two sons and prayed for them while they were soldiers. She had not feared deportation because she never felt she had done anything wrong. But confinement in a nursing home had been the ultimate blow. It seemed Maria Antonia had lost her will to live. So, she began to withdraw. One staffer suspected she had begun hiding her food in her pockets instead of eating it, which would explain why she had lost noticeable weight in the time she was a nursing home resident. Had Anita López not surprised her one day at the facility, she would not have seen for herself how much her grandmother's independent, fearless character had declined. This time, when she pushed her grandmother's wheelchair to her assigned room, she did not even sound the same. In fact, once she helped her get into her twin-sized bed, she told Anita not to say the usual "patas arriba" that had always made her burst out laughing. Instead, she asked Anita to prepare for her impending death, when she was sliding Maria Antonia's frail body across the mattress.

Anita mia, my Anita. You have helped me as much as you can. This body can no longer carry its own weight. I am so tired. I am tired of living here. Being here has made me tired of living. It's time for me to go. I don't think we'll see each other again.

In Spanish, and attempting to make abuelita feel better, Anita told her grandmother:

Don't say that abuelita! I'll talk to the staff to make sure a doctor comes to see how you're doing and to check your blood pressure. The doctor can check your heart and give you medicine for your arthritis. You will feel better once a doctor sees you.

Rather than hear the intent of her message and the love Anita carried for her inside her heart, abuela affirmed the value of her grandchildren in her life.

I loved all my grandchildren, but you were special. I don't blame you for anything that happened. I just want all of you to look after Minerva. She will need your help. Minerva cannot get by alone. She was a special child who wanted to design her own way in life.

Maria Antonia whispered in Anita's ear, speaking for the first time in the past tense as she lay on her bed,

She was my only daughter, and she was often contrary, obstinate and belligerent. Yet I never gave up hope that one day she would see I had loved her. That she would one day realize I had spent my life trying to help her. I have forgiven her judgmental attitude toward me. Remember, that at the end of our lives only God can judge us.

Anita López felt helpless. She could do no more than listen. Here was her grandmother evaluating her daughter's lifelong antagonistic behavior. As always, the unconditional love she felt for her daughter prompted her to give Minerva the benefit of the doubt. Regardless of how hurtful her treatment had been, abuelita excused all of Minerva's transgressions.

Anita López told abuela that she had taught her to forgive so that she too would forgive her mother and her half-sister Martha who had hurt so many.

"Abuelita, gracias a ti yo también se cómo perdonar. Así que si tú la perdonas, yo la perdono a ella y a mi media hermana que me ha hecho tanto daño a mí y a mucha gente."

Tearfully, she kissed her grandmother on the forehead and cheeks more deeply than she had ever kissed her before. Her heart sank as she closed her eyes, hanging on Maria Antonia's every word. In her heart of hearts, she knew this would be the last time she saw her beloved grandmother alive.

Four months after her visit to Michigan, Anita López received the phone call she had been dreading. Hilda Zonlak called her to tell her Maria Antonia had passed away in the presence of her three surviving children. All three had coincidentally gone to visit her at the nursing home on what would be her final day. Hilda told her that she had peacefully passed, while seated in her wheelchair listening to her adult children speculate about why she had been rushed to the hospital for a simple case of constipation—she bowed her head and slipped away. Beto rushed to get a nurse, but she was pronounced dead before an ambulance arrived.

As soon as she could, Anita López bought a ticket to Michigan. Maria Antonia's funeral arrangements were perfectly handled by Hilda Zonlak—a Catholic mass drew many family members, and a bilingual priest gave a thought-provoking eulogy.

At the services, Minerva Castañeda Peña spontaneously launched into a song, as the crowd looked on in wonder. She had not consulted any family member or the priest. And since she had never had a good singing voice, she was sadly and embarrassingly out of tune.

The pallbearers included Beto, two grandsons, and three great-grandsons that lifted the casket taking it out to the garden cemetery where she would be laid to rest. Everyone followed the casket outdoors singing De Colores, a familiar religious Spanish song, which caused many to weep.

The funeral ended with a family gathering that included generous amounts of food. All the piping hot plates of enchiladas, tacos, tamales, carne guisada, guacamole, and red and green mole were lovingly prepared by the wives of Maria Antonia's sons, their daughters, and granddaughters.

Anita did not think the word matriarch described her abuelita accurately. Yet no one could deny Maria Antonia's life and example had had a profound generational impact on her entire family. Her four children had grown up, worked, and achieved independence under her guidance. The three witnessing her passing would not forget many of her colorful expressions such as, "¡Dios me favorezca! May God favor me" and her teachings.

Maria Antonia had often heard fellow immigrants say the United States was the only country of opportunities. But she had learned that worth as a human being in the United States was tied entirely to a person's monetary value, and she'd often say,

> When you have no money and no property, nobody values you. That's why I always say: "tanto tienes, tanto vales." Your worth depends on how much money or property you have. In this country or anywhere, if you don't have money or your own property, you have no value.

Referencing the deplorable conditions she and other Mexican immigrants experienced during their seasonal trips to work in California, Florida, Ohio, Wisconsin, and Michigan, Maria Antonia would say,

> Somos pobres pero limpios, meaning we may be poor, but we're clean. Just because some people have more than others doesn't mean they are better human beings. Like I always say, "no todo lo que brilla es oro" or not all that shines is gold.

Another motto that her children and grandchildren heard daily and would remember included, "No hay que tener vergüenza por el trabajo. Debemos estar orgullosos de nuestro trabajo y de que aún trabajamos," or "never be ashamed of the kind of work you do, instead be proud of your work and that you have work."

Anita López never forgot the story her grandmother told her about the way in which Anglo store owners looked at her and her children when they went into their stores. She said they looked down on them because her sons wore bib overalls and she and her daughter wore blue jeans.

> Los bolillos or the Anglos stared at us and followed us around the store as if we were going to steal something. We went to buy necessities. My children and I always had cash. But they treated us as if we were thieves. They didn't care that we were paying in American dólares.

She also recalled abuelita telling her,

> Even other customers looked at us. The onlookers stared suspiciously because the boys wore blue jean overalls, and Minerva and I wore pants. We dressed like that because we had just finished working in the fields. But even when we went to Sunday Mass wearing our best clothes, they looked down on us.

Most memorable for her descendants was the way Maria Antonia extolled the merits of embracing a strong work ethic. Work hard, from sunup to sundown if that's what it takes to survive with dignity and self-respect. Yes, money was desperately needed but earn it; don't beg for money or take handouts, she would insist.

Now, WITH HER PASSING, Maria Antonia's senior-citizen children would experience life without their mother's sage advice. Three years later, Jeorge Castañeda would join his mother. Minerva Castañeda Peña would soon follow but not before enduring and surviving unimaginable physical trauma. She had become accustomed to daily medication for diabetes. But a urinary tract infection forced Minerva to visit a local doctor. Throughout her life, she had stayed away from doctors as much as her mother. The two had always placed great faith in natural remedies, and on faith healer curandera recommendations. Some homemade potions had worked in the past. So it was with great apprehension, and at her daughter's urging, that Minerva agreed to allow a doctor to examine her, when Gina Peña Schmidt pleaded,

> Listen to me mom, you had diabetes for a long time before you were forced to accept it. You went without medical attention for so long you harmed your kidneys. This urinary tract infection could be dangerous. You should let a doctor check to see why it hurts to pee.

Minerva Castañeda Peña listened, allowing Gina to take her to a local doctor. Two weeks after taking prescribed medication for the infection, Minerva had a horrific allergic reaction. This resulted in a condition called Stevens Johnson syndrome, an unusually adverse reaction that had been masked by a high fever, a cough, and breathing difficulty.

It was Gina Peña Schmidt who found her mother unresponsive and lying on the floor of her rented mobile home. When she saw the hideous sores on her legs and arms Gina screamed. At the local hospital, the family was informed that this was a life-threatening medical condition because of diabetes and age. The reaction could be fatal.

Minerva Castañeda Peña, like her mother, had avoided doctors. She had not called her daughter until she felt the sting of painful blisters and burns over much of her body. From Midland, she was rushed to a hospital that specialized in treating burn victims in Ann Arbor, Michigan, where she spent three weeks in intensive care. Medical staffers heard her blood-curdling screams while her body was submerged in a whirlpool and painstakingly scrubbed back to health.

When Minerva Castañeda Peña abandoned her mother in San Antonio and moved back to Michigan, Gina Peña Schmidt had voluntarily taken over Minerva's affairs and helped sell her house. She had found her mobile home and persuaded her to stop driving when she saw her vision had declined to near blindness. Her mother had always been stubborn but was forced to now rely on her completely. Aware of her mother's inability to budget, Gina Peña Schmidt had even agreed to handle her social security check. She paid her monthly bills, bought her medicine and food, and ensured she had enough left until her next check arrived. Gina had spent countless hours on the telephone calling social services and Medicare to ensure her mother was enrolled in services designed for the elderly. All of this she had done while holding down a full-time job and tending to the needs of her own family. Gina told Anita López,

> I've done everything I can to help her. I don't know why she reacted so badly to the prescribed medicine for a urinary tract infection. Mom looked horrible. We've never seen anything like this. She has burns all over her arms, legs, and torso.

She added, speaking about abuelita's and her mother's distrust of medical doctors,

> You see, that's why mom and abuelita have always refused to go to doctors. Mom always said they're too eager to cut you open, when you go in with an ailment. And, if she dies from this medication, we need to sue the doctor who gave it to her.

After months of rehabilitation, however, Minerva survived the worst experience of her adult life. Daily exercise at a physical therapy center helped her regain enough strength to walk with a cane. And while her case was severe, she did not require surgery. Unfortunately, her newfound health was short lived. Family members commented that they were glad Maria Antonia was no longer around to see her deteriorating condition. Gina Peña Schmidt began calling all family members to say Stevens Johnson syndrome had deteriorated her immune system. That, coupled with diabetes, had taken a toll on her frail body. Because Minerva's kidneys and liver were on the verge of collapsing, the doctor transferred her to a hospice facility near Gina's home to await impending death.

Mercedes López, Julián Peña, and Eva Peña lived nearby and were the first visitors to tell their mother goodbye. Martha López and her husband drove in from Tulsa, Oklahoma. She knew this might be the last time she'd see her mother alive. Still, Martha's warlike personality led to a confrontation. Alarmed by the harsh words with which she spoke to Minerva, shortly after her arrival, the staff asked Martha to leave.

Anita López was the last of her six children to arrive in time to speak to Minerva. She didn't dare let on that she knew her kidneys and lungs were failing. Minerva Castañeda Peña's voice was softer than usual. Her mother didn't talk as if she knew what it meant to be in a hospice. Unaware or in denial that she was in an end-of-life facility, Minerva said,

Anita, I'm so happy you came back. There is so much I want to say now. You know I need to stay in this place until I get better. The blisters on my body have healed and started to fade away, so I can go home now.

Anita continued the conversation, opening a discussion regarding Minerva and Maria Atonia's mother and daughter relationship.

I've been wanting to talk to you about me and Toña. You always asked why my mother and I didn't get along. Well, you knew I resented her, but you never knew why. Well, I'm ready to tell you why, she said holding her daughter's hand for the first time ever.

Anita López had always yearned to be as close to her mother as she was to abuelita. She had wished for her kiss, her hug, or just a gentle touch. Since that had never happened, she had grown accustomed to her coldness. Of course, she was surprised by her mother's warmth and willingness to speak candidly, thus Minerva began,

I held a grudge. I blamed her because I was raped when I was twelve. She had left me alone in a shack for almost two days while she went to pick cotton a few miles away with my brothers. She should have known someone might break in and hurt me.

Minerva continued calmly at first but gradually began raising her voice.

God was merciful to me because I did not get pregnant, and that was only because I had not yet started menstruation. I didn't even know what menstruation was! Toña never told me. I started after that horrible incident, but I thought my uterus had been damaged for life!

In response to Minerva's disclosure, Anita replied,

I wish you would have told us, mom. Maybe we could have understood why you seemed to resent abuelita all those years. None of us ever understood why you didn't call her mamá. Or why you didn't seem to love your own mother. We thought you even hated her!

She continued disclosing the contradictions that had emerged in their mother daughter relationship.

Toña had told a neighbor I didn't like working in the fields. She asked her if she'd keep an eye on me. While I was alone in that old shack farmers used to provide for migrant workers, a man broke in. I tried to fight him! For the rest of my life, I felt so ashamed. I never told anyone, not even Toña!

Minerva Castañeda Peña never told her secret to anyone in the family. She had kept it to herself and became even a more quiet and painfully shy child. Because she feared her mother, she never said what she was thinking. While a strict disciplinarian, Maria Antonia never hit her. At school, she never spoke unless spoken to. Minerva felt devalued and unloved, and she continued,

I always felt she loved her sons more than she loved me, especially my brother Jeorge. She never told me about things girls need to know, like menstruation. That's why when it happened to me one day, I cried. I didn't know what was going on. Toña brushed off my humiliation by saying it was a natural fact of being a female.

Once she married her first husband, Minerva Castañeda Peña resolved to challenge anything her mother said. She tried to place the shame and fear behind her, simultaneously putting a lifelong wedge between them.

Minerva Castañeda Peña survived her bout with Stevens Johnson syndrome. After months of physical therapy, she returned to her mobile home unaware she was dying. Minerva was convinced she could beat diabetes by ingesting her basket full of vitamins and herbs. The thought of moving on reenergized her. She returned to writing children's books. Having published one, she was determined to write more. There was no limit to her imagination. In Spanish, her nursery rhymes were as good as those of the famous Mother Goose rhymes. In English and Spanish, she wrote poetry and short stories.

She also expressed the surprising desire to return to her Roman Catholic upbringing. Anita López was shocked to hear her say that. She wondered if her older sister, Mercedes López, a lifelong devout Catholic, had had anything to do with her mother's sudden re-conversion to Catholicism. She told a speechless Anita López, during a visit,

I'm so happy Mercedes left Washington, D.C. That city was not good for her. Here in Midland, she has everything. The Catholic church is within walking distance, and I go with her most every Sunday now.

The family was overjoyed and relieved that Minerva's hospitalization and physical therapy had led to a speedy recovery, because no one in the family would have volunteered to tell Maria Antonia that she had lost her daughter. God mercifully spared her life so she could attend her mother's funeral later that year.

MARIA ANTONIA died at the age of one hundred and six. Her funeral drew a throng of family members, some of whom were total strangers to Anita López. There were few friends left to attend her funeral; she had outlived most of them. At her celebration of life, grandchildren talked about how she had impacted them. Great-grandchildren said they had heard Maria Antonia had true grit, and that she was proud of her Mexican heritage. Although her great-grandchildren didn't know her well enough to speak to her, Maria Antonia spoke to them in Spanish.

"Aprendan Español. Learn Spanish. Es un idioma muy importante. It is a very important language," she would say. They simply nodded and replied. "Sí. Abuelita." These were the only two words most of them had learned in Spanish.

During Maria Antonia's lifetime the language she had spoken all her life had grown tenfold to include more than five hundred million people worldwide. The language her children were forbidden to speak on the playground in Dallas schools had become a global triumph. Her children, grandchildren, and great-grandchildren had heard it all. They had heard about how she had arrived after the Mexican Revolution. They had learned how she and her children had endured widespread discrimination in the United States. They also found out about her unwavering patriotism, when she scolded those youth who were disrespecting the flag.

Yes, we were discriminated against many times here in this country. But the reason I still salute the flag and love this country is because I am grateful to the United States for giving me and millions of Mexicans refuge after the revolution.

Abuelita Maria Antonia taught her retoños about other types of discrimination she confronted. She told them,

Not all discrimination we lived through was racial. I'll never forget we were mistreated when we went into a store dressed in blue jeans. That was economic discrimination. But since Beto and I have lighter skin, we were not racially discriminated against like Jeorge, Paco, and Minerva.

With an amiable personality, Beto Castañeda never knew a stranger; he didn't have a mean bone in his body. Perhaps that is why fate was kinder to him. He remained married to his high school sweetheart his entire life. He died at the age of ninety-two, surrounded by his children, grandchildren, and great-grandchildren. Preceded in death by his older siblings, those who knew Beto and loved him wished he had lived to be a centenarian like his mother. Some relatives recalled how he had danced away the night at his last birthday party at the age of ninety-one.

At the funeral, Beto was the first to eulogize Maria Antonia. Despite his mother's death, he made a valiant effort not to shed tears of profound sadness. He had been guided by her wisdom and received her spiritual advice all through his lengthy marriage. Like his brother Jeorge, Beto visited Maria Antonia in San Antonio almost every summer. Since he had inherited an aptitude for carpentry from his uncle Fulgencio Menchaca, Beto used his vacation time to patch up windows, doors and anything else Maria Antonia's house needed. At her celebration of life, Beto proudly told the crowd,

> My mother was the salt of the earth. There was nothing she couldn't do if she had to do it. I saw her pick cotton in the hot Texas sun. I picked tomatoes and potatoes alongside her in several states. She even climbed trees to pick cherries in Traverse City, after we established residency in Michigan.

Mary Vega Castañeda, his wife of more than sixty years, applauded her mother-in-law's courage; her indomitable spirit. She admired the way in which she had singled-handedly raised her three sons to be hard working responsible American citizens. She especially appreciated how she tolerated and helped her daughter. Mary said,

> She did a wonderful job raising her family all by herself, and it wasn't easy in those days. And she was determined that they would be hard workers. She always said she didn't want them in gangs or growing up to be bums.

Mary made no comments about Minerva, even though all recalled and understood the ways Minerva Castañeda Peña disrespected Maria Antonia, after all she had done for her. The couple's oldest daughter, Lisa Castañeda Garza, stepped to the podium after her parents. Anita López was pleasantly surprised by what Lisa said, holding up a pink baby shawl Maria Antonia had made for Lisa when Mary was pregnant with her.

> Abuelita was the most thoughtful, loving grandmother ever. She crocheted this and gave it to my mother while she was pregnant with me. I kept it for my own daughter who was born twenty-five years ago. This is a gift of love that I have cherished my whole life. Now that abuelita is with God, it is even more meaningful.

Lisa had inherited her father's jovial personality and his Spanish looks, including the most beautiful emerald, green eyes in the family. She had stunned her mother, Mary Vega, for no one on her side of the family was born with green eyes. Lisa Castañeda Garza had always admired how hard working her father had been throughout his life. He was such a great father and family man that he inspired her to find a husband just like him. Finally, she credited her grandmother for raising him to be the man he was.

Lisa was followed by others. Handsome grandson, George Castañeda Jr. talked about how she had spoiled him from birth through his teens. Although she had moved to Texas while he was a teenager, George never forgot her advice on dating, marriage, and raising children. "Abuelita always hugged and kissed me a lot. She spoiled me so much, and she'd give me whatever I asked for. I think it's because I was the only boy in the family," said the chemical engineer who had followed Mercedes footsteps by graduating from Michigan State University.

His mother, Gloria Zapata Castañeda said that Maria Antonia had taught her all about cooking, baking, sewing, knitting, and the art of crocheting, and even had helped her nurse and raise her seven children. At the funeral, Gloria recalled,

I was very young when I married her son Jeorge and I had lost my own mother as a teenager. I knew nothing about housekeeping, not even how to cook. But she knew how to cook, how to sew, how to make things, and I learned everything I know from her.

Most of those in attendance expressed gratitude for Maria Antonia's sage advice about daily life, and the guidance she doled out on the importance of saving money and paying off a home quickly for a mortgage-free life. They admired that Maria Antonia had consistently spoken in Spanish to her adult children. During the years she had lived with Jeorge and Gloria, her grandchildren became fluent in Spanish.

Those in the younger generations pointed out that as they began growing up and going to school, the Spanish language was replaced with English. Still, several grandchildren were glad that Maria Antonia kept speaking to them in Spanish, whether they understood her or not.

Julián Peña, who was one of the pallbearers at her funeral said,

During the short time she lived with us, she thought I was making fun of her for not speaking English ... But when she spoke to me in Spanish, I laughed because she knew I didn't understand her, yet she kept talking to me anyway.

Everyone who spoke said that Maria Antonia had impacted their lives in a host of positive ways. That was when Anita realized that Maria Antonia's life and legacy had transcended generations. She recalled that Maria Antonia at her final birthday party had compared her descendants to sprouts retoños and that there wouldn't have been any descendants in the United States had she and her husband not emigrated. "Todos ustedes son nuestros retoños. Si no hubiéramos dejado a México, no habría ningún retoño aquí en los Estados Unidos."

Maria Antonia Menchaca Castañeda left an impressive legacy of perseverance, self-reliance, and determination. She was a great example for her retoños or spouts. Because of her love for flowers and plants, and her use of Spanish words to describe buds or saplings when referring to her grandchildren and great-grandchildren. Some heard the word retoños for the first time that day.

Sadly, on a return visit to Maria Antonia's gravesite, Anita López learned that they had buried abuelita in a segregated Catholic cemetery. Although Anita had been at the mass and funeral, she had not noticed that. When she told family members how surprised she was to see this on her first visit since abuelita's death—they were not angry. They simply said that being surrounded by other family members and many Mexican friends was a testament to their community. She had not acquired the impregnable strength she carried from having survived the revolution alone. Long before the warring factions exploded among the diaspora of Mexican people, Maria Antonia was a fiercely independent child. She strongly believed that her resolute spirit was decidedly genetic, and that the other part could be attributed to her rural and rugged upbringing. Maria Antonia coming to terms with her innate traits had helped family and friends understand why she evolved into a fearless entrepreneur and champion of the downtrodden. Also, her character made Maria Antonia a conduit for the troubles of some family members whose burdens she eased with compassion, advice, and money.

Maria Antonia never hesitated to tell anyone that she lived through various wars in her country, as well as survived those in which her sons fought for the United States.

To encourage those who were still coming up, she'd often say, "Let me tell you, at ninety I showed the strength to assist in building a flight of wooden stairs in my dilapidated San Antonio home. In my early twenties, I demonstrated the capacity and strength to establish a storefront business." With these words, it was her intent to show her retoños the possibilities in life, concluding with, "When I set my mind to do something. I get it done!"

Sources

De Leon, A. (1983). *They Called Them Greasers: Anglo Attitudes Towards Mexicans in Texas 1821-1900*. University of Texas at Austin and Texas State Historical Association www.tshaonline.com.

Hill, N. (1937). *Think and Grow Rich* by as read by Earl Nightengale (radio personality) in phonograph record circa 1950s Napolean Hill Foundation www.napolean.org

McElhaney J. and Hazel M. V. (n.d.) Texas State Historical Association https://www.tshaonline.org/handbook/entries/-dallas-texas

Mercado, B. (2008). *With Their Hearts in Their Hands: Forging a Mexican Community in Dallas 1900-1925*. B.A. Master of Arts Thesis at the University of North Texas. www.digital.library.unt.edu/ark:/

Simek, D. P. (2018). Lost Dallas the City's Forgotten Past and Untold History Magazine www.dmagazine.com/micropost/kera-nonprofit/publica-tions/d-magzine/2018/

Velasquez, L. S. *Stories of the Mexican Revolution, www.Frontera.neh.gov/*closer readings.

Mexican Revolution

The Mexican Revolution: Causes, Summary & Facts. www.britannica.com

Mexican Revolution, 1910-1946. Oxford Research | Latin American History. https://www.oxfordre.com

The Mexican Revolution: November 1910-NEH-www.edsitement.neh.gov/ closer readings.

Stories of the Mexican Revolution www.Frontera.Library.UCLA

Mexico News Daily https://www.mexiconewsdaily.com

About Adelitas: Who were the Adelitas during the Mexican Revolution| www.inside-mexico.com.

Las Soldaderas: Women of the Mexican Revolution www.soldaderas.omeka. net. The Los Angeles Public Library https://www.lapl.org

Instituto Nacional de Estudios Históricos de La Revolución de México https://in-ehrm.gob.mx/work/models/

Library of Congress Research Guides Mexican Revolution: Topics in Chronicling America.

History.com www.history.com/news/operation-wetback

Basques or vascos in Mexico

Los vascos de México https://www.losvascosdemexico.org.

Inmigración Vasca en México https://es.wikipedia.org/wiki/inmigracion_vasca_en_mexico

Los vascos immigrated to Mexico from 1810-1910 https://euskonews.eus

Los vascos en el México Decimonónico 1810-1910 by https://www.kosmopolita.com

History of Texas and Dallas

Texas Our Texas www.texaspbs.org The Great Depression and World War II/great-depression-ww2.

Mirror View History of Dallas, Texas A Journey Through Time www.mirror-view.com/history-of-dallas-a-journey-through-time.

History of Dallas (1930-1945) en.wikipedia.org/wiki/historyofdallas209

A look at Little Mexico Dallas Historical Society www.dallashistory.org/event/a-look-at-little-mexico

Dallas Mexican American Historical League https://dmahl.org

Dallas Nonprofit Gathers Stories of Mexican Americans Who Helped Build the City https://www.wfaa.com/article/news/local/la-vida/dallas-nonprofit-gathers-stories-of-mexican-americans-who-helped-build-the-city.

Preservation Dallas www.preservationdallas.org/location/ Pike Park Recreation Center (Little Mexico) 2807 Harry Hines Boulevard Now Uptown.

Somos Primos (n.d.) online website focusing on Latino/Hispanic History Contributed by Academics, Journalists and Historians. https://www.somosprimos.

Rosario (Rosie) Carbó is a former newspaper reporter whose work has appeared in many Texas newspapers, including The Dallas Morning News. An award-winning print journalist, her feature articles have appeared in national magazines and online publications. A graduate of the University of North Texas, she earned a Bachelor of Arts in Journalism. Carbó is a former member of The Society for Professional Journalists. She also attended law school and became a member of Phi Alpha Delta. *Maria Antonia y Sus Retoños: Legacies of Motherhood* is based on the life of her beloved maternal grandmother.